Jameal,

You are blessed because your walk is in step with the Lord, you delight in His Word, and meditate offering praises to Him day and night; you will continue to yield fruit in every season.

Thanks, Psalm 1:1-3

Manifestations of God's Word

5/10/23

LaKeesha Griffin
also known as "God's pupil"

Copyright © 2022 LaKeesha Griffin
Cover Design and illustrations by Ezekiel Griffin, II
All rights reserved.

No part of this book may be reproduced in any manner whatsoever without the prior written permission of the publisher, except in the case of brief quotations embodied in reviews.

The views and opinions expressed in this book are those of the author and do not necessarily reflect the official policy or position of Halo Publishing International. Any content provided by our authors are of their opinion and are not intended to malign any religion, ethnic group, club, organization, company, individual or anyone or anything.

ISBN: 978-1-63765-279-4
LCCN: 2022914138

Halo Publishing International, LLC
www.halopublishing.com

Printed and bound in the United States of America

To my husband and three beautiful children,

Thank you for the daily experiences that heighten my senses and challenge me to see God's glory in it all.

Introduction

Have you felt spiritually isolated even though you are religiously connected? Oftentimes, as believers, we go religiously through our day-to-day hoping that through daily activities, we will feel closer to God. We mistake our good works for how connected we should feel to God. We do our best to do the absolute right thing so we can hear Him, see Him, and feel Him in our lives. We go to church and attend Sunday School, Bible Study, church events, small groups, and the like to feel more connected. We often find this routine causes us to feel more disconnected and more isolated.

It is not by chance that Jesus chose parables to communicate to His people. He knew that by meeting His people where they were, they would be able to relate and, in turn, really comprehend the Word of God. Jesus chose our daily occurrences to foster Biblical revelation. It is such a beautiful truth that God almighty humbled Himself and made Himself small so that we could really understand Biblical truths.

After being very active in church but still feeling disconnected, God revealed to me His Biblical truths through my hurt, pain, sorrow, and trials. Like many of you, I tried my very best to be exceptional in all I did. I went above and beyond for every role I played, whether it was as a wife, mother, daughter, sister, friend, church member, and so on. Despite me striving for perfection in these many roles, I became seriously ill—I was suffering from an autoimmune disease that affects every area of my body, most particularly my lungs. I had one diagnosis after another—inflammation around my heart, growths in my lungs, a tumor on my brain, just to name a few. I began to question why and why me. I was angry that despite doing everything I had been taught a good Christian should do—acting selflessly and always taking care of others, no matter what I lacked—I was severely sick. It was in my deepest sorrow when God spoke to me.

You see, I had suffered a great deal to get where I was. I had become an attorney despite the odds, leaving my newly purchased home and taking my entire family— my husband and two children—in pursuit of fulfilling my childhood dream. At five years old, I had role-played being an attorney with my brothers. As I got older, that desire to become an attorney deepened as I became more familiar with injustices. When faced with the choice to pursue my dream or continue on the path I was unhappy with, I chose the former, and I was willing to leave everything behind to get there. What a blessing it was that my husband agreed to follow me and uproot our children for my pursuit of happiness.

My husband and I both started professional school. He pursued a degree in occupational therapy, and I pursued my juris doctorate degree to become an attorney. We went through a lot to make it, including moving in with relatives and commuting two hours to school every day with our two preschool children. So, after all I had scarified—working tirelessly to pursue a profession and being active in church and community outreach—I did not understand my plight. Why was I always sick? When I stood tall, why did I get knocked back down? And my most consistent questions: where was God in all this? Why did I feel so disconnected?

It was there, in my deepest sorrow, God spoke to me. As I cried to God that I felt like a burden to my husband because of my sickness and questioned Him on what to do now, God met me where I was and said, "Write." It was by my obedience that my eyes were opened to the question I asked God in the midnight hours of my tears—"Where are you?"

God's reply to my question was, "Everywhere." God allowed me to see that He manifests Himself in our daily occurrences. He reconciled my hurt, pain, sorrow, and trials with His Word. I realize now that I was never alone and that I was always connected to Him. Most importantly, through it all, He revealed to me my true love—writing. Now, I look for His manifestation in everything I do, knowing He will reveal His Biblical truths throughout my daily occurrences, which in turn will reveal to me more about my God-designed purpose and identity.

I consider it a joy to have suffered to see God as plainly as this. It is my hope that my words, which were given to me by God, will be a spark for you to feel as connected to God and His biblical truths. I hope to be a catalyst for how you see God through your everyday occurrences. "For in Him we live and move and have our being."[1]

---

[1] Acts 17:28 (NIV)

Biblical Roots for Your Week

Week 1

Hope brought something new that allowed for an escape from the past and gave rise to clear vision for the future—an opportunity renewed daily.

Renewed Hope

At the beginning of all things, there are new opportunities. This is felt across the world as we celebrate a new year. With a new year, oftentimes we make new goals, commonly referred to as our New Year's Resolutions. But most of the time, those resolutions become daunting tasks, and several months from the onset of a new habit or attempting a new goal, we get discouraged, too busy, and/or disinterested and give up.

I, my husband, and our three children have a New Year's Vision Board Party every year. It is so funny to see my youngest son think about the required four things he should put in each category. Why? Shouldn't it be easy to just jot down what you desire for yourself? Not always. You see, we are not only required to think of at least four things for each category; most importantly, we must also set a realistic timeframe or deadline. We laughed so hard as my son read his list of resolutions and wrote on his board that within a few days, per his timeframe/deadline, they were to all be completed. Funny, right! But we are no different. We often operate in this same vein, wanting everything to be done quickly and over fairly soon. But it takes time to do the necessary work to meet a sincere goal.

I am reminded of a saying we have in our kitchen: "If God didn't do it in one day, neither can I." I hope this resonates with you as it does with me. It is not that God was powerless to create everything in one day; instead, He chose to focus His attention on a few things at a time. On the first day, God created time, light, heaven and earth; on the second day, God created the sky and seas; on the third day, God created the land and plants; on the fourth day, God created the sun, moon, stars, and planets; on the fifth day, God created the fish and birds; and on the sixth day, God created animals of the land and man.[2] Then, on the seventh day, God finished His work and chose to rest.[3]

It is my belief that our most powerful God was setting the standard we should live by when engaging in the "newness" of anything: focus your attention on a little at a time, and then sit back and rest to see the glory of how it all worked

---

[2] Genesis 1:1–31
[3] Genesis 2:2

together to create something new. Yes, we should tackle our goals, but too much too soon is a recipe for defeat. Instead, give each goal a realistic timeframe for completion and then tackle it (work) with the respective faith it takes to see it to fruition because your mountain(s) can only be removed with the requisite faith in God.[4] In Mark 11:22, Jesus said, "Truly I tell you, if anyone says to this mountain, 'Go, throw yourself into the sea,' and does not doubt in their heart but believes that what they say will happen, it will be done for them."[5]

Our takeaway is then this: to meet our goals with success, do a little at a time with faith, and do not forsake the blessing of rest!

LaKeesha Griffin, God's pupil

Prayer

Lord, the Great Architect, I, (put your name here), thank you that everything you made is perfect. I thank you that in your plans for all of creation, you had a perfect plan for me. I thank you that those plans include an abundant life. Lord, thank you for my vision. I know my vision for my life is God-instilled. Now Lord, I repent that I have been overzealous with getting to success. I often cloud the vision you have given me with an earthly desire to be on top. I repent that I have not followed your perfect framework in how I should work towards my goals, which is to do a little at a time with faith and not forsake the blessing of rest. I realize that if I never rest, I will never have an opportunity to assess, like

---

[4] James 2:26
[5] James 2:26 (NIV)

you did, that what I am working towards is good and very good. Lord, I ask you to help me stay diligent, yet obedient to the design for life you have left me. Now, Lord, here I am, willing and able to do your will, and work the plan. In Jesus's name, Amen.

Application

1. What vision are you working towards?

2. Are you being reasonably diligent towards that goal, incorporating rest and an assessment period? Or are you burning the midnight oil, working tirelessly to reach your goal?

3. Re-write your vision to include a rest and assessment period.

4. Now, be intentional about changing your timeframe/deadline so that it includes rest and an assessment period.

5. Remain open to God's direction on achieving your vision.

Make Notes Here:

Biblical Roots for Your Week

Week 2

To find rest despite being in the midst of chaos is what the soul truly requires.

The Soul's Rest

The word "rest" is a verb, which means it requires an action. "Rest" is, therefore, something we must do. Most people think of "rest" as moments of inactivity. The dictionary defines "rest" as what we do when we cease doing the work or movements so we may relax, refresh, or recover strength. However, "rest" is also a noun. Nouns are used to identify people, places, or things. The Bible identifies "rest" as Jesus.

In Matthew 11:28–30, Jesus teaches that He is our "rest." He says, "Come to me, all who are weary and burdened, and

I will give you rest. Take my yoke upon you and learn from me, for I am gentle and humble in heart, and you will find REST for your souls. For my yoke is easy and my burden is light."[6] Jesus is teaching us that the "rest" we are looking for is not in our moments of inactivity or when we decide to take a break. Instead, it is when we identify Jesus as our "rest" and take the action of coming to Him. Only by coming to Him will we find "rest" for our souls. This is the real "rest" we desire and need: "rest" from our thoughts, past, addictions, heartache, pain, fears, worry, and so on.

Newton's first law of motion tells us that an object at rest stays at rest, and an object in motion stays in motion unless acted upon by an unbalanced force. It continues that object (just like people) keep on doing what they are doing unless acted upon by an unbalanced force. Jesus is the unbalanced force because His power is incomparable. He is the force we all need to act upon us so we can arrive at real "rest" and stay at "rest." He is what we need to keep us from doing what causes our soul to always be in motion.

Identify Jesus today as the "rest" you need for you soul.

LaKeesha Griffin, God's pupil

Prayer

Lord, I, (put your name here), acknowledge that you are the "rest" for my busy soul. Thank you for always being there for me, never leaving me nor forsaking me. I am caught, Father, in the continual race of life. I am tired, Lord. I need you to take this burden from me. Give me the "rest" that only you can provide. I know with that "rest" I will find peace for

---

[6] Matthew 11:28–30 (NIV)

my soul, a peace which surpasses all understanding. Help me to walk in your light, Lord, so I may follow your footsteps to eliminate the constant pressure I place on myself to accomplish everything in one day. Lord, I acknowledge that you yourself did not create all creation in one day, nor can I accomplish all of life's demands and tasks in one day. Lord, I acknowledge that you displayed my need for "rest" when you, after finishing your work, rested as well. Lord, I come to you repenting that I have not been intentional to "rest." I ask for your forgiveness, and I receive it now. Now, Lord, here I am, willing and able to do your Will and "rest." In Jesus's name, Amen.

Application

1. Identify what causes you to be so busy that you deny yourself "rest."

2. Prioritize what is a necessity rather than placing pressure on yourself.

3. For those things that are necessities, find someone you may delegate some things to or share the load with.

4. For those things that you identify as pressure you place on yourself, either eliminate them altogether or spread them out over a reasonable time.

5. Designate a time throughout the day to "rest" and completely detach from worldly concerns.

6. Designate a day throughout the week to "rest" and detox from the stresses of the week.

7. Be intentional to keep praying for God to reveal the areas you should cast upon Him to relieve your burdens.

Make Notes Here:

Biblical Roots for your Week

Week 3

If God sings over me in admiration despite the complexities of my life, then why, too, can't I?

The Gift of Song

We all have that one song that boosts our spirit when we are having a bad day, our prospects are few, or our bank account is depleted. That song boosts our morale because the words speak directly to our hearts. God gave us this gift—the gift of song. David was inspired by song. This is evident in his Psalms, many of which we have turned into hymns or gospel music. Jesus himself believed song to be a strong gift from God.

In Matthew 26:26–30 (NIV), Jesus and the disciples share the last supper. He tells them after breaking the bread, "Take and eat; this is my body." Then He takes the cup, gives thanks, and offers the cup to the disciples, telling them, "This is my blood of the covenant which is poured out for many for the forgiveness of sins." After Jesus and the disciples partook of the last supper, scripture tells us they sung a hymn.[7] Many believe that the hymn they sung comes from Psalms 115–118.

Psalm 115 (NIV) says, "Not to us, Lord, not to us but to your name be the glory, because of your love and faithfulness.[8] Psalm 116 (NIV) says, "I love the Lord, for He heard my voice; He heard my cry for mercy." Psalm 117 says, "Praise the Lord, all you nations; extol Him, all you peoples. " Finally, Psalm 118 (NIV) says, "Give thanks to the Lord, for He is good, His love endures forever."

Although we do not know the exact song Jesus and the disciples sung after the last supper, we know from these Psalms that it was a song about God's love and faithfulness, His mercy, how He is a God for all people, and that His very nature is good. In other words, it was a song about God's character. Any song that reflects God's character can revive the downcast and their outlook on their perceived hopeless situation.

I encourage you to sing your song. God has gifted it to you to remind you that what you see and feel right now is not a reflection of who you are or where He is taking you. In fact, He has so much more in store for you. David knew God had more for him as he was hiding from King Saul in the cave; David knew it wasn't the end for him because he knew the true value of God's love for him.[9] Scripture tells

---

[7] Matthew 26:30 (NIV)
[8] Psalm 115 (NIV)
[9] 1 Samuel 24:3–4

us that David's journey didn't end there, and he later sang[10] and even danced before the Lord.[11] You, too, are purposed for something greater because of God's love for you.

So, SING! Make a joyful noise unto the Lord!

LaKeesha Griffin, God's pupil

Prayer

Lord, Creator of all things, I, (put your name here), thank you for being so wise to know how important the gift of song would be for me to revive my downcast soul. I acknowledge that all good things come from you, Father. And I thank you for this gift of song. I will be intentional, like David, to sing to you, Lord, so you may get the honor and glory. Lord, you deserve my absolute praise. I am reminded that singing to you is a twofold benefit: it is a time when you receive your due praise and when I am reminded of your character. I acknowledge that your character is love. And because you are the very essence of love, you always love me unequivocally. Therefore, despite the trials I face, I realize your love is enough. So, I choose today to make a joyful noise unto you, Father. I know your love never fails me, and because of that love, my destiny doesn't end here. Now, Lord, here I am, willing and able to do your Will and "sing." In Jesus's name, Amen.

---

[10] 2 Samuel 22:1
[11] 2 Samuel 6:14

Application

1. Identify the hymn, gospel song, or Christian music that overwhelms you with emotion and hope but, most importantly, honors God.

2. Sing that song to God.

3. Dance before the Lord.

4. Make singing and dancing before the Lord a habit, especially when you feel downcast.

5. Be intentional to keep praying to God about His Will for your life: ask God to reveal to you your purpose and His plan for you.

Make Notes Here:

Biblical Roots for Your Week

Week 4

When I want what I want and someone else requires something different of me, let me choose the latter.

Remaining Flexible like Christ

One of the hardest things is when we have an agenda, a goal to reach, a plan of things to be done, or a problem to be resolved, and then some other issue or problem is introduced, delaying our set date or timeline for when our goal is to be reached or problem is supposed to be solved. When this happens, it forces us to adjust. Oftentimes, this causes anxiousness because, as an old adage says, our plate becomes too full. Now, we are juggling more than what was initially expected. In times where we can't get to the root of one issue because another one pops up, we have to remain flexible.

Jesus Himself led His life here on Earth to show us it is a necessity to have a disposition of flexibility. Jesus would have a mission in mind for where He was going, then, while on the way, someone would plead with Him to heal them. Jesus would always adjust His mission, being flexible to bless those He encountered. It was a regular course for Jesus to stop what He was doing to bless someone.

In Matthew 9:18–22, Jesus was on His way to restore the life of a synagogue leader's daughter, but He was willing to delay this mission in order to heal a woman suffering from 12 years with an issue of blood. In John 11:1–6, we see Jesus, being fully aware that His dear friend Lazarus was sick with impending death, decide to then stay where He was for two more days to carry out His mission there. In Matthew 19:13–15, Jesus was teaching to a large crowd; despite that, people still brought little children to Him so He could pray blessings over them. The disciples rebuked them, but Jesus welcomed it, saying, "Let the little children come to me, and do not hinder them."[12] Jesus was always willing to be flexible in the moment for the sake of those coming to Him in need. He was confident that the delay in His mission was a way for God's glory to prevail. One example of God getting the glory, despite the delay, is when Jesus raised Lazarus, who had been in the grave for four days, from the dead. When we are thrown off course and can't seem to implement our plan, let's be willing to prioritize what's important.

Let's be flexible to change our plans for the need of others. Let's accept that our delays are a way for God's glory to prevail.

LaKeesha Griffin, God's pupil

---

[12] Matthew 19:14 (NIV)

Prayer

Lord, the Most Compassionate One, I, (put your name here), thank you that you do not hide your face from me. I thank you that you never reject or forsake me. I thank you that you are always willing to stop what you are doing and render help to me in my time of need. You are faithful to receive me in my desperation. Thank you for showing me how to be flexible and prioritize the needs of others. Lord, I repent that I have not prioritized the needs of others if they conflict with my schedule. I repent that I fail to see that helping others when I am busy is a requirement for Kingdom living. Please forgive me, Father, for not being willing to stop what I am doing, like you so graciously do, to help another in need. I ask you to help me see what the priority is for the Kingdom of Heaven to prevail. Now Lord, here I am, willing and able to do your will, and help others in need despite the busyness of my schedule. In Jesus's name, Amen.

Application

1. Think back on a time when you were overwhelmed with tasks to meet a deadline, and someone asked you for help.

2. How did you respond to their request for help?

3. If you helped them, did you do it begrudgingly? If you didn't help them, why not?

4. Now, remember a time when someone stopped what they were doing in their busy day to help you. Where would you be if they did not,

or what would have happened if they refused to help you?

5. Continue to pray that God helps you put the needs of others first.

Make Notes Here:

Biblical Roots for Your Week

Week 5

To be socially accountable is to use words to revive the sunken soul.

Sharing Your Power

Have you ever been on your way to somewhere, gotten everything in your car—maybe your purse, bag, or even groceries—and put your key in the ignition only to be disappointed that your car will not crank? It throws you for a loop, especially when it was working earlier that day. If you are like me, you are completely in disbelief that it's not working; so, you turn the ignition again, but to no avail. Now you are faced with diagnosing the problem and, most likely, finding the temporary fix for the problem.

If you turn your key and find that the lights or radio are trying to come on, you deduce that it's a battery problem, and you need your battery charged, or a "jump off." Someone—a good samaritan or even a family member or friend—will then use jumping cables to transfer energy from their battery to yours. They're not transferring it all—just enough that your car may be of use. They are sharing their "power." This is analogous to the power of our words.

Oftentimes, people endure life on a "low battery"—they are barely getting by with life and its circumstances; then, suddenly, they become completely stalled. Our words then have the "power" to revive that person. Like the transfer of energy from a "jump off," we, too, can share our energy through our words so that someone with a "low battery" may continue their life and be of use to the Kingdom of God. Proverbs 18:21 (NIV) says, "The tongue has the power of life and death." 2 Corinthians 10:4 says, "The weapons we fight with . . . have the divine power to demolish strongholds." I encourage you to share the "power" God has given you to revive those around you suffering from a "low battery."

Be encouraged that you have the "power" to speak to the dry bones so that they will live and live with more "power."[13]

LaKeesha Griffin, God's pupil

Prayer

Lord, the Omnipotent Father, I, (put your name here), thank you that you are all-powerful and that your power reigns in all situations. You can revive the dry bones, or the low battery I am enduring in my life, and cause me to live, and to

---

[13] Ezekiel 37: 1–14

live with power and more abundantly. I acknowledge that I am just toiling through life, going through the motions because I feel that it is what I am supposed to do. I acknowledge that this toiling causes me to feel drained and lifeless. Lord, you are the only one who can restore me completely to working in full power. I repent, Lord, that I have not allowed the power that raised Jesus Christ from the dead to work in me. I repent, Lord, that I have not yielded to your power. I yield now and surrender to your power so that my power may be restored. Lord, I ask you to help me be someone who always lends a kind hand and a healing word to those who also may be suffering from a low battery. I repent that I have not always used my words for your glory, but I choose to do that today and every other day of my life. I acknowledge that I have the power to demolish strongholds. I will speak with power and authority not only in my life, but over the lives of others. I will speak to the dry bones, knowing that my faith will erect the lifeless. Now, Lord, here I am, willing and able to do your will and let you restore my power. In Jesus's name, Amen.

Application

1. Identify what causes you to suffer from a "low battery."

2. Categorize each into headings, whether it is money, marriage, and so on.

3. Find at least two scriptures for each heading.

4. Demolish strongholds with your words by speaking those scriptures with authority over the things you have written in the respective heading.

5. Make this a continual practice and watch God break the strongholds.

6. Be intentional to speak words of encouragement to charge the "low battery" in others' lives.

Make Notes Here:

Biblical Roots for Your Week

Week 6

To choose to see the desert as a place to harvest is great perspective.

Opportunity in the Desert

"Desert" is a word with multiple meanings. When used as a verb, it means to abandon in a disloyal way. Scripturally, it means to leave or forsake. When used as a noun, it refers to a dry, barren place that is desolate and often without what is required to sustain life. Sometimes, we feel like we are in a desert with no access to the things we need to sustain the life we have.

Our relationships, finances, career opportunities, and so on may seem desolate. But when it seems like all is lost and there is no help in sight, God responds. God sends help in our dry places. In Genesis 16:1–11, Hagar ran into a desert from a situation she felt she could not endure; after having conceived a child with Abram for him and Sarai, per Sarai's request, she was now being treated harshly. Though she was near a spring in the desert, she could not see any hope in her desert. She could not perceive the new thing God was doing in her life. Then, an angel appeared and revived her hope for a future. The angel told her that God had heard her affliction.

God will always send help in our deserts. We just have to give our afflictions to Him and ask for eyes to perceive what He is doing in our lives. In Isaiah 43:18–19, God instructs, "Remember ye not the former things, neither consider the things of old. Behold, I will do a new thing; now it shall spring forth; shall ye not know it? I will even make a way in the wilderness, and rivers in the desert."

Ask God to open your eyes to the "new thing" He is doing in your life. He will never desert you in your desert! He will never leave you nor forsake you!!!

LaKeesha Griffin, God's pupil

Prayer

Lord, the God who sees me, I, (put your name here), thank you that you never leave me nor forsake me. I thank you that you chase after me in my desolate places. Lord, I have often felt all alone and without any help. I repent because I know now that I felt isolated because I was looking for help from man instead of you, the God who sees me. Lord, you are my help. Lord, you are my sufficiency. I thank you that not only do you see my physical location, but you see the state of my heart and where I am struggling in my soul. I give, Lord, my afflictions to you. You know them all, even the ones I don't acknowledge. So, I am confident that you will do a miraculous thing in me, despite my afflictions. Now that I have given you my afflictions, Father, I ask that you give me eyes to see the new thing you are doing in my life. I know that you are paving a path for me that has never been walked on before. I know you are making a way in my desert. I choose to see the spring in my desert. I choose to hope for my future because you, Lord, are my hope and confidence. Now, Lord, here I am, willing and able to do your will and let you make rivers in my desert. In Jesus's name, Amen.

Application

1. Sit with your eyes closed in a quiet room, completely alone, and resolve within yourself that you are not alone, but God is there.

2. Have an honest conversation with God about your desert—not only are you talking, but you are being intentional to listen to God.

3. Ask for eyes to see the new thing God is doing in your life.

4. Be intentional to see your desert differently and to see new opportunities and provisions right where you are.

5. When rivers flood your desert, acknowledge that your desert is God-designed and give Him the glory.

Make Notes Here:

Biblical Roots for Your Week

Week 7

While toiling around this circle of life, let me not forget to focus on its center.

The Centermost Point

A circle is a shape in which we can't tell its beginning or its end. For a circle, all of its points are an equal distance from its center. Let me ask you a question: have you come full circle?

This adage is often meant to express that one has returned to his/her original position, or there is a complete reversal of something. Thus, you coming full circle could apply to a multitude of things in your life. You could have been toiling away at getting a degree, and now you are finally working in your craft. You may have started a new business, and now you are seeing fruit from your labor. You may have received a grim diagnosis from your doctor, and now they are saying you have been miraculously healed. You may have had problems in your marriage or have been in deep prayer about a wayward child, and now blessings abound in your marriage, or your child is living a life pleasing to the Lord. In all examples, even the one you are living right now, each one (all of its points) has a common center. Yes, you guessed it! Like the beautiful gospel song, Jesus is at the center of it all. But let's take a moment to talk about the most important full circle you can experience.

In Revelation 2:1–7, Jesus sends a letter of encouragement to the Ephesus church. Jesus first points out what they have done well: "I know your deeds, your hard work and your perseverance."[14] Then He acknowledges their trials, struggle, and heartbreak: "You have persevered and have endured hardships for my name, and have not grown weary."[15] But Jesus charges the Ephesus church, and He is charging us who continue to go through the routine without remembering who they are doing it for: "You have forsaken the love you had at first."[16] Jesus then encourages us to make a full circle and return back to our first love: Him. He says, "Turn back! Recover your dear early love. No time to waste, for I'm well on my way to removing your light from the golden CIRCLE."[17]

Sometimes in the circle of life, we get caught in the motion (the loop) and forget the purpose of it all; we forget the center of it all, the center who is holding it all together—Jesus. Jesus

---

[14] Revelation 2:1 (NIV)
[15] Revelation 2:3 (NIV)
[16] Revelation 2:4 (NIV)
[17] Revelation 2:4–5 (MSG)

is telling us He can bring us full circle—a complete reversal of our situation or heightened growth and fruitfulness in an area we may have be struggling with—if we just return unto Him. I encourage you to remember your first love!

LaKeesha Griffin, God's pupil

Prayer

Lord, My First Love, I, (put your name here), thank you that you are at the center of everything I face or could possibly face in life. You hold me throughout every situation. You see to it that there is an ending to my pain, struggle, trial, and hardships. Lord, you see to it that my circle revolves around you and evolves for you. Lord, I have not always begun what I am facing with you in my focus. I know that if I look to you, help is coming, and that you will manifest bringing the thing I am facing to a full circle. I thank you that you are at the center of it all and that you are holding me by my right hand. I repent now for failing to acknowledge you in the process of what I am doing. I repent that I have been just going through the motions, this loop of life, without the passion I first started with. That passion, Lord, is you. Lord, I ask, since I can do nothing without you, that you help me return back to you, My First Love. Now Lord, here I am, willing and able to do your will and return unto you. In Jesus's name, Amen.

Application

1. Write down a narrative of your experience when you accepted Christ as your Lord and Savior. Make sure to write every feeling you felt at that moment.

2. Write down some of the things you did for the Lord out of pure love for Him.

3. Honestly answer this question: are you doing what you do now out of obligation (people expect you to do it) or pure love for Christ?

4. Make a plan to disengage from the things you are doing just for obligation; then, make a plan to just spend time with God so that your love for Him is renewed.

Make Notes Here:

Biblical Roots for Your Week

Week 8

My tears and pain are necessary for my growth as the rain is required for the thorny roses to bloom.

Recycling Tears

To "recycle" is to convert something for the purpose of it being reused again. The "key" to whether something is recyclable is whether it has the potential to repossess the properties it had in its original state. God is the "master recycler." He converts the trash in our lives—our sins, disobedience, and wayward thinking and living—into something He can use. Romans 8:28 (NIV) encourages us "that in ALL things God works for the good of those who love Him, who have been called according to His purpose."

ALL means the good and the bad—including the moments we show lack of reverence to God, when we disobey and obey, when we fail to defer to His wisdom and when we do, and so on. So, since ALL encompasses every moment of our lives, how can the bad be used for our good? Simply put, it is because God recycles our bad and turns it into something good.

Isaiah 61:3 (NIV) tells us how God recycles our mourning and grief by bestowing on us "a Crown of beauty instead of ashes, the oil of Joy instead of mourning, and a Garment of Praise instead of a spirit of despair." He too teaches us that we can recycle our pain by sowing it back to him—"They that sow in tears shall reap in joy."[18] Well, what about the "key" to recycling?

When we have fallen in sin, do we still have the potential to repossess the properties we had before we sinned? "Yes, of course!" Our God, the "master recycler," is telling you today, "Behold, I make all things new."[19] It doesn't matter how many times we fall; He recycles our sin and makes us new. "This means that anyone who belongs to Christ has become a new person many times. Again and again, God gives us a new start, a new life—the old life has gone; a new life emerges!"[20]

So, the real "key" to recycling is whether we belong to Christ. In other words, the "master recycler" only recycles the junk that belongs to Him. Give your junk to Christ today!

LaKeesha Griffin, God's pupil

---

[18] Psalm 126:5 (KJV)
[19] Revelation 21:5 (KJV)
[20] 2 Corinthians 5:17 (MSG)

Prayer

Lord, the Master Recycler, I, (put your name here), thank you that you choose to make me new again and again, despite my shortcomings, sins, and, oftentimes, disbelief. You are a faithful God. You are faithful to bring to completion the work that you have started within me. I love you, Father. I know my love for you is incomparable to your love for me, but it at least puts me in a position to receive the good you have in store for me so that my junk can be recycled. Lord, I repent for all my junk—the misplaced anger, complaints, and disobedience. I want to be better, Lord. I want to be better so that you can get the glory out of my life. I willingly give my junk to you today. I ask for a complete makeover. Lord, make me over spiritually, emotionally, mentally, and physically. If you find anything that is unreflective of you, purge it away from my heart, and replace it with what is pleasing in your sight and a sweet fragrance unto your nostrils. You have my permission to recycle me infinitely. Now, Lord, here I am, willing and able to do your will and allow you to make me what you desire for me to be for the glory of your kingdom. In Jesus's name, Amen.

Application

1. Openly acknowledge the parts of your life that you know are unreflective of God's Word.

2. Continue to pray about those areas of your life that you feel displease God by asking Him to change your environment and/or circumstances or take away bad habits and addictions.

3. Write a list of all the things you do exceptionally well—i.e., writing, singing, advocacy, teaching, or even a sport.

4. Devise a plan on how you can do those things so that God can get the glory, then do them.

5. Be open-minded to changing your plans when God gives you an assignment to do more or do something else entirely for His glory.

Make Notes Here:

Biblical Roots for Your Week

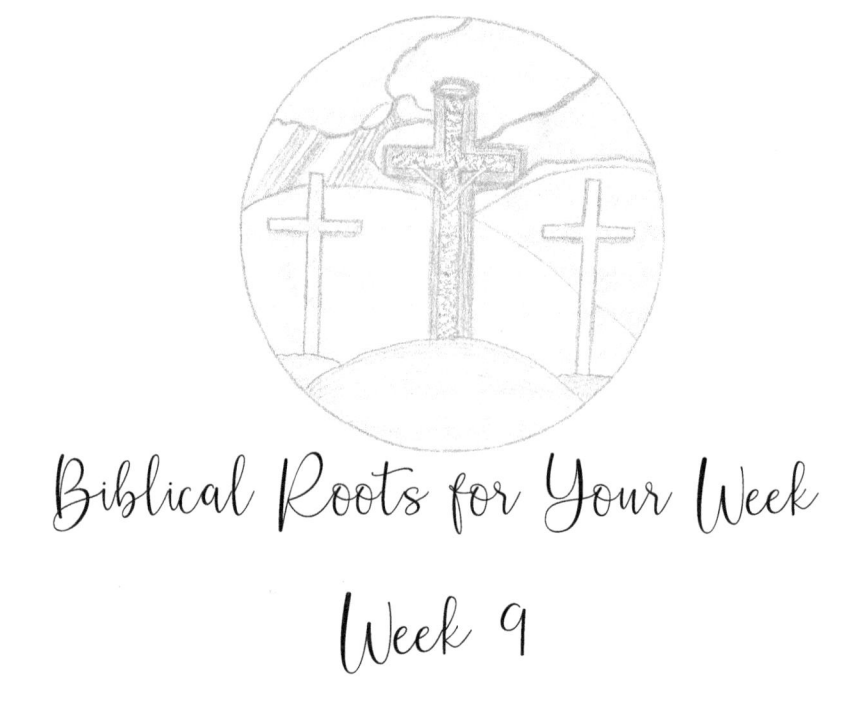

Week 9

When I look in the mirror, my reflection is not my own, it is God's.

God's Reflection

If you sit still long enough, you will recognize and feel God's glory all around you. God's glory is in everything—the trees and the seasons; the wind and how it feels like God Himself is passing by; the sun and rain in how they cause new growth; even the storms in how they bring about new opportunities to start afresh. God, in His infinite wisdom, created light (first day); the sky (second day); land with vegetation and the seas (third day); the sun and moon (fourth day); birds to fill the sky and fish to fill the waters (fifth day); and animals (sixth day). But God didn't stop there; He then created man (sixth day).[21]

We often look outwardly for signs of God's glory. However, we should look inwardly because the creation of man is the greatest example we have of God's glory.[22] He made you, me, and even the coworker or family member that tests your patience, in His own image. No other creation reflects God's image. Now, this doesn't mean we look like Him, but it means we "look" like Him. Well, what does that mean? That means we don't physically look like Him because God is a spirit, but our character or our love and behavior toward God's greatest creation (man) is a reflection of Him. Genesis 5:1 (NIV) says that God made us in His "likeness." In other words, we always carry the potential to reflect God's nature.

In Exodus 34:6 (NIV), God proclaims Himself to be compassionate, gracious, slow to anger, abounding in love and faithfulness, loving, and forgiving. So, when we operate in that very same nature, we look like God, hence His "likeness." I purport that we are God's greatest creation because we are His only creation in which He can see Himself.

I ask you, are you looking like God? Just like a child dressing up in his dad's clothing and modeling his dad's behavior, so should we. He has clothed us with garments of salvation and robes of righteousness; He has placed His likeness within us.[23] Don't you want to look like your Heavenly Father?

LaKeesha Griffin, God's pupil

---

[21] Genesis 1:1–27
[22] Genesis 1:27
[23] Isaiah 61:10 (NIV)

Prayer

Lord, my Creator, I, (put your name here), thank you for creating me in your own likeness. I thank you that you love me enough to grace me with your nature. I thank you that you have always been compassionate, gracious, slow to anger, abounding in love and faithfulness, loving, and forgiving toward me. Lord, I recognize your glory in your creation. I realize now that the greatest example of your glory is me, because in me, I can see you. I also realize I reflect you when I am acting in your nature toward your greatest creation, man. Lord, I repent that I have not chosen to wear my garments of salvation and robes of righteousness. I repent that my nature has been too much of a reflection of the world, like being envious, greedy, selfish, and lusting after the rewards of the world instead of my eternal reward. I choose to wear my garments of salvation and robes of righteousness henceforth. Like you, Lord, I will choose to show compassion and grace. I will be slow to anger, even when others clearly oppose me and try to hurt me. I will walk in love and faithfulness. I will love and forgive. Lord, I ask that you help me with this and to be a great example of your glory. Now, Lord, here I am, willing and able to do your will, and show the world your glory. In Jesus's name, Amen.

Application

1. Write down the consistent challenges you may face in your daily routine—i.e., dealing with a bothersome co-worker, family obligations, and so on.

2. Identify how you may not be reflecting God's nature in your reactions to those challenges.

3. For every bad reaction, write an example of how you can react differently and reflect God's nature as being compassionate, gracious, slow to anger, abounding in love and faithfulness, loving, and forgiving.

4. Continue to pray and ask God to allow your reactions to your daily challenges to align with His nature.

Make Notes Here:

Biblical Roots for Your Week

Week 10

My regrets fostered my maturity, and my maturity found my faith, and my faith secured my standing.

The Beauty of Right Now

If you are like me, you can pinpoint a moment or moments of regret. Perhaps there was a decision, in hindsight, you now know you should've made. Maybe you even wish you would have taken an alternative route to where you are now, because now you know that alternate route would have saved you heartache and pain. However, you also may be like me in that you realize if not for your past, you would have never reached your "Aha" moment. That is, if not for your pain, heartache, and struggle, you would not have the relationship you have with God; in other words, you wouldn't be as mature in Christ.

All too often, when we look back on our past, our hearts become entangled in the what-ifs. Our regrets of missed time and failed feats can often keep us from the beauty of our reality or the promises of our near future. Would you believe it if I told you that looking back can be as detrimental to you as what you thought you missed out on?

Lot's wife, who was instructed by God via the angel to not look back, indeed looked back, and consequently, she turned into a pillar of salt.[24] As God was destroying Sodom and Gomorrah for their sins against Him and each other, God instructed Lot and his family not to look back.[25] It was God's intent to spare Lot's wife from destruction and death, but she could not keep herself from looking back.

It is my belief that she turned into a pillar of salt not only because she physically looked back, but more so, she couldn't keep her heart out of the past. She could not see the new thing God was doing; instead, she only saw regret in what God was trying to make her past. God demands that we forget those things behind us, reach toward what is before us, and "press toward the mark for the prize of the high calling of God in Christ Jesus."[26]

The purpose of Lot's wife was unfulfilled. We never even learn her name because she is not named in the Bible. What is baffling is that God chose to turn her into salt ("You are the salt of the earth. But if the salt loses its saltiness, how

---

[24] Genesis 17:26
[25] Genesis 12:17
[26] Philippians 3:13 (KJV)

can it be made salty again? It is no longer good for anything, except to be thrown out and trampled underfoot.")[27] I believe He chose to turn her into salt to remind us that although He has good intentions toward us, we can never fulfill our purpose as long as our hearts are in the past and we fail to see the beauty in right now.

I encourage you, "Don't Look Back!"

LaKeesha Griffin, God's pupil

Prayer

Lord, my Hope and Future, I, (put your name here), thank you that your plans for me will prevail. I thank you that you have plans to prosper me and not to harm me. I thank you that my hope and future are secure as long as I continue to put my trust and confidence in you. Lord, I have thought too much about the what-ifs. I have regretted so many of my choices. I have often felt that I missed my purpose, my calling, because I chose a wrong path. Lord, I repent now that I have not chosen to see the beauty in right now. Lord, I repent for failing to acknowledge that your hand is on my life and in the plans for my life. Lord, I ask that you open my eyes to see how you have beautifully orchestrated my life. Now, Lord, here I am, willing and able to do your will and ceasing to live in regret. In Jesus's name, Amen.

Application

1. Write down the one regret you play over and over again in your head.

---

[27] Matthew 5:13 (NIV)

2. Write down how you think your life would be different if you made a different choice.

3. Now, write a list on all the things you would have missed out on if you never made the choice(s) you made—i.e., you never would have met a special person; you never would have experienced something memorable, and so on.

4. Pray about your regrets and give them to God, then resolve to see the beautiful gifts God gave you despite your choice(s).

Make Notes Here:

Biblical Roots for Your Week

Week 11

Eloquence of speech is most successful when it captures the heart of man and their souls for Christ.

Recommend Christ

An "elevator speech" is a quick personal pitch about yourself, an idea, or a business proposal you may have. It is a mini-commercial, normally 30 to 60 seconds or around 75 words, about you or your plans and is directed at someone with decision-making power. We have all seen an "elevator speech" on television where an enthusiastic, eager person synced their timing to be on an elevator with someone who can make their dreams come true, hence the term "elevator speech." The reason why these speeches are so short is because, yes, the elevator ride is brief, but also because one can capture the attention of the person who is receiving the speech in a short time, factoring in their attention span, busyness, unwillingness to talk with you without an appointment, and so on.

An "elevator speech" is what believers should craft to get the attention of unbelievers. In Matthew 28:19, we are blessed to receive the "Great Commission." Jesus said to the disciples to multiply the discipleship: "Therefore go and make disciples of all nations, baptizing them in the name of the Father and the Son and the Holy Spirit, and teaching them to obey everything I have commanded you."[28] Jesus does not dictate how long each encounter should take; in fact, he leaves it up to us to be creative.

Jesus is the perfect example of one who gave "elevator speeches." Jesus spoke in parables, which are extended analogies, or earthly stories with eternal implications. His parables were indeed short stories with a spiritual lesson, hence the comparison of an "elevator speech."

Given that we all have been called to the "Great Commission," think closely on how to capture the attention of unbelievers. Like Jesus, be crafty with your words. The unbeliever can ultimately make the decision, but you can influence it with your words!

Go and make disciples of all nations!

LaKeesha Griffin, God's pupil

---

[28] Matthew 28:19 (NIV)

Prayer

Lord, you are the Word; I, (put your name here), thank you that you were there in the beginning of time, and you are present now. I thank you that you walked on this earth and are familiar, even empathetic, with the human condition and our hearts. Lord, you were crafty in your words, getting unbelievers to turn to you, even to be a disciple for God's kingdom. I thank you that your words have pierced my heart, and there I hide them so that I do not sin against you. Lord, I repent that I have not done my very best to speak to unbelievers about your works, wonders, and miracles. Lord, help me to share the Gospel with your people and to take the Great Commission seriously. All I want is for my actions to be pleasing in your sight. I know that if I choose to be intentional to break the barrier between the believer and the unbeliever, then I will, with your help, win souls for Christ. Now Lord, here I am, willing and able to do your will and go make disciples of all nations. In Jesus's name, Amen.

Application

1. Write down your elevator speech.

2. Practice your elevator speech so that it is short and quick to grab the attention of the unbeliever.

3. Go out and make disciples of men for the Kingdom of God.

4. Pray that everyone you come into contact with and profess the Gospel to will receive Christ as their Lord and Savior.

Make Notes Here:

Biblical Roots for Your Week

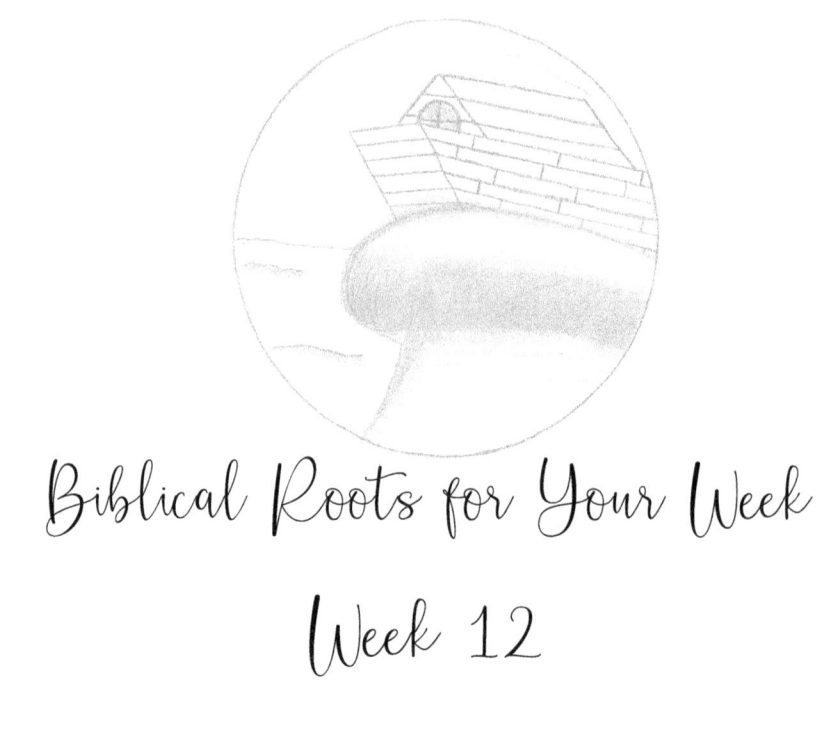

Week 12

The ratio cannot be quantified when God is in it!

The Immeasurable

A "ratio" is the quantitative relationship between two things showing the number of times one thing is within the other. In other words, a "ratio" equals the relative value of two things. We see a "ratio" often talked about in the classroom setting; for example, there is one teacher for every so many students. But God is not limited by the concept of a "ratio." We see examples of this all through scripture.

In Matthew 14:14–20, Jesus saw a large crowd and had compassion for them, healing their sicknesses throughout the day. Late in the day, instead of Jesus sending them away to find their own food, he made provisions for them with what little they had—five loaves of bread and two fish. Scripture tells us that with the five loaves and two fish, more than 5,000 were fed; it was about 5,000 men without counting the women and children who were also fed.[29] The "ratio" for Jesus can be "undetermined"—five loaves: more than 5,000; two fish: more than 5,000—and He can still leave you with more than enough. Scripture tells us that there was a "remainder" of 12 basketfuls left over.[30]

Jesus did this awesome thing of feeding a large crowd one more time in scripture—he made provision for a crowd of 4,000 men with the number of women and children being fed not counted.[31] There was an "undetermined ratio"—7 loaves: more than 4,000; a few small fish: more than 4,000. There was also a "remainder" of seven basketfuls left over.[32] The commonality between both scriptural events is that Jesus is intentional to give thanks before the distribution.[33]

What can we learn from the "undetermined ratio"? Whatever you have—even if it does not seem like enough to pay the bills, get out of debt, feed your family at the moment, and so on—be intentional to give thanks before the distribution, and then watch God give you the "remainder" from the "undetermined ratio." You'll see the God of more than enough, Jehovah Jireh, take your situation/circumstances and make provisions to leave you with basketfuls.

Don't wreck your brain trying to figure out the "undetermined ratio"; instead, give thanks to God for it, and then

---

[29] Matthew 14:21
[30] Matthew 14:20
[31] Matthew 15:32–38
[32] Matthew 15:37
[33] Matthew 14:19; Matthew 15:36

open your hands to receive the basketfuls of provisions from the "God of remainders!"

LaKeesha Griffin, God's pupil

Prayer

Lord, my Jehovah Jireh and God of Remainders, I, (put your name here), thank you that you provide even when I have little resources. I thank you, God, that you are a God of provisions, and you delight in multiplication. With you there is no lack because your grace is always sufficient. Lord, I repent that I have only recognized your provision in my life in hindsight. I have failed, Father, to walk confidently knowing that though I am in the midst of a struggle, you have already worked it out. I repent of my tears of despair. I know now, Lord, that there is nothing too hard for my God. When you provide, there is always something left over. I will bask in your grace and be confident that I will see an outpouring of your provisions in undetermined ratios. I open my hands, Lord, and receive a life of abundance from you, My Provider. I ask you to help me walk in faith and not by sight. Help me see the glass as half full instead of half empty and to not grow weary in my wait for your rescue. Now Lord, here I am, willing and able to do your will and wait on my miracle that has an attached remainder. In Jesus's name, Amen.

Application

1. Write down at least one time God showed himself to you as Jehovah Jireh when you had limited resources.

2. Be intentional to share that testimony with someone else so that God may get the glory.

3. How would your life be different if you put your complete trust in God as your sufficiency?

4. Pray for a peace that transcends all to guard your heart and your mind as you resolve within yourself to trust God wholeheartedly.

Make Notes Here:

Biblical Roots for Your Week

Week 13

I am bestowed an abundance of grace to be seen beyond my lies.

Free from Condemnation

Can you remember the first time you told a lie? Probably not. We learn from our environment at an early age how to manipulate the truth. Maybe our first lie was when we blamed something we did on our sibling or when we ate the cookie we weren't supposed to eat. One way or another, we got used to bending the truth to get what we wanted. It became easier and easier with time.

Lying can be as easy as riding a bike. But have you ever fallen off a bike and gotten bruises and scrapes? Sometimes doing something that seems natural is the wrong thing because it leaves us with bruises and scrapes. Lies leave us with guilt and shame. And guess what—lies are intended to work that way!

The Word of God tells us that lies are from the devil, because he is the father of lies; in fact, it goes in depth to say that lies are the devil's native tongue.[34] I purport to you that lies are the devil's manifestation in our lives. But no matter what little white lie we told, truth we omitted, or big lie we are afraid to confess because it will get us into deep trouble, God will forgive us. Not only will He forgive us, but the Holy Spirit also testifies that the Lord says, "Their sins and lawless acts I will remember no more."[35]

It is amazing that the one we sin against wipes our slate clean and frees us from all condemning charges against us.[36] He takes our guilt and shame (bruises and scrapes) and teaches us how to live for Him. The Word says He renews our mind, for inwardly we are renewed day by day.[37] But God doesn't just stop there! What we destroyed with our lies, omissions, and deep, dark secrets, God reconciles.

God reconciles the estranged parent to the child, the distant (only talking at the family reunion) siblings, the heartbroken spouses, and the friends who fell out of touch due to some misunderstanding. God can heal all wrongs and reconcile any relationship. Most importantly, He can reconcile us back to Him, and He takes great delight in it.

In the game of chess, you have to make the right moves to knock down the obstacles (pawns, etc.) in your way. God is

---

[34] John 8:44
[35] Hebrews 10:17 (NIV)
[36] Romans 8:31–34
[37] 2 Corinthians 4:16 (NIV)

the master player of chess. He knocks down the obstacles in our way, even if the obstacles were created by us, so we can assume our rightful position as royalty. In other words, He knows all the obstacles you have to endure; He knows how to make you who He created you to be; and most importantly, He knows how and when to checkmate your opponent. God is saying, "Checkmate!"

LaKeesha Griffin, God's pupil

Prayer

Lord, the Champion of My Life, I, (put your name here), thank you that you are the master player of this chess game called life. I thank you that you know how to turn my wrongs into right. I thank you that you move my wrongs out of the way so I can get to my rightful place in your Kingdom. I thank you that you continuously chase after me in such a loving way. You never give up on me, even when my deceitful ways bring shame and separation into our relationship. Your steadfast love always reconciles me back to you. I truly love you, Father. Lord, I repent that I have lived dishonestly. I have used deceit to get my way and justify my point. I was more concerned about my ego than my relationship with you. Lord, please forgive me for acting uncharacteristic of your Kingdom. I thank you that though I have stumbled, I have not fallen because you uphold me. I thank you that my position in your Kingdom is unchanging because you, the master player of this chess game called life, fight for me, have died for me, and intervene for me. Lord, I ask you to help me walk with integrity and confidence and to throw away deceit. Now, Lord, here I am, willing and able to do your will and live truthfully. In Jesus's name, Amen.

Application

1. Acknowledge the deceitful behavior of your past and confess your sins to God.

2. Write at least one person's name you can share your confession with. ("Therefore confess your sins to each other and pray for each other so that you may be healed." James 5:16 (NIV))

3. Confess your sins and pray with the person you identified as a confidant, and charge them with the task of keeping you accountable.

4. Pray about it if guilt or shame arise, then walk in victory because your sins have already been forgiven.

Make Notes Here:

Biblical Roots for Your Week

Week 14

Punishment meant for one and taken on by another is redemptive love.

Redemptive Love

Do you have a sibling? If you do, you probably know what it feels like to be punished for doing something you didn't do; instead, your sibling was the guilty one. Did the sibling confess to their wrongdoing? Most likely not! Why risk getting punished when your brother/sister can take the blame for you? Maybe instead it was a cousin. Or even now, maybe it is a slothful co-worker.

It is never a good feeling to suffer the punishment meant for someone else. But you know what, Jesus said before Our Father: it wasn't them, it was me! Rarely do you see a sibling confess to their wrongdoings instead of allowing the innocent brother/sister to be punished. Often co-workers won't fess up, either for fear of losing job security or just having poor integrity. But for someone to knowingly take the blame and guilt for another when they are completely innocent is baffling. This is what Jesus did for us; "the punishment that brought us peace was on Him."[38]

Jesus knew the importance of God's plan for us, though He also knew the magnitude of pain of our sins on His body. He prayed that the cup be taken away from Him; yet He still yielded to God's plan.[39] Jesus, who was spirit born in flesh, signed our guilty verdicts, and the list of charges were infinite (present, past, and future sins). He willingly bore them at the cross. He took our guilty verdicts and had them nailed to the cross, where they would remain if we would just call upon Him. Jesus said to His Father: It was not them, it was me! He knew His blood carried the only redemptive, cleansing power to save God's children.

Rarely do you find a love so great as that required to willingly take on the guilt of others. But there is only one who could take on the guilt of the world and wash them clean. And guess what? Jesus is glad He did it. What a love!

Our convictions have been pardoned by the blood of Jesus! Hallelujah!

LaKeesha Griffin, God's pupil

Prayer

Lord, my Savior, I, (put your name here), thank you that you bore my sins. I thank you that when you were nailed on the

---

[38] Isaiah 53:5 (NIV)
[39] Luke 22:42–45

Cross, you were actively nailing my past, present, and future sins to the Cross as well. I know there is no greater expression of love than when you laid down your life for mine. I thank you that because all of my sins are nailed to the Cross, I, too, can be resurrected. My hopes, dreams, relationships, health, and finances can all be resurrected from the grave because you rose from the grave with all power after having paid for all of my sins. Thank you, Lord, for saying, "It wasn't them, it was me!" Thank you for yielding to God's plan for my life. Lord, I repent that I have not taken your sacrifice seriously. I often forget the pain and suffering you bore for my freedom. I ask you, Father, to keep me mindful of your sacrifice in all that I do. Now Lord, here I am, willing and able to do your will and live forever cognizant of the gift of redemption you gave me. In Jesus's name, Amen.

Application

1. Write down a time when you suffered or were punished at the fault of someone else who escaped blame.

2. Write down a time when someone else suffered or was punished at the fault of you, who escaped blame.

3. Now, resolve within yourself that Jesus paid for the faults of you both, and forgive that person and yourself: Lord, I forgive myself for (insert what you did without blame here). Lord, I forgive (insert the person who escaped blame here) for (insert what that person did here).

Make Notes Here:

Biblical Roots for Your Week

Week 15

Being rooted in God's Word fortifies strength to survive the approaching storms.

Deeply Rooted

Erosion is the process that removes soil, rock, or dissolved material to a new place. "A tree planted by a river" is susceptible to erosion. Not only does the movement or flow of the water erode the soil around "a tree planted by a river," but the harshness of bad weather (rainstorms, tornadoes, tropical storms, and hurricanes) causes the surface soil to be moved to a new place.

Erosion is a non-factor to a deeply rooted tree. No matter the storm, a deeply rooted tree withstands! Psalm 1:1–3 (KJV) describes one who delights and meditates on God's

Word as "a tree planted by the rivers of water." The psalm goes on to say that this tree is unaffected by the season—this "tree planted by a river" continues to bring forth fruit in his/her season; its leaf does not wither; and whatsoever he/she does prospers.[40] But how can a "tree planted by a river" be fruitful despite the elements going against it? Easy; it's deeply rooted.

In John 15:5 (KJV), Jesus tells us that He is the vine, and we are the branches. Only by abiding in Him can we bear fruit. He goes on to warn us that apart from Him, we can do nothing.[41] So the only way we can withstand the elements of life (hardships, career changes, sickness, death of a loved one, etc.) is by being "a tree planted by a river" that is connected to the vine (Jesus).

He is our "roots" in any and all situations. Abide in the one true vine; without Jesus, all our attempts wither, but with Him, we bear fruit in perpetuity. Don't go into the storm alone!

LaKeesha Griffin, God's pupil

Prayer

Lord, you are the One True Vine. I, (put your name here), thank you that you have chosen to abide in me, and because you abide in me, and I chose to abide in you, I am fruitful. I thank you that in you I grow. I acknowledge that I am maturing in Christ not by my own doing, but by everything you place within me. Lord, I repent that I have often tackled a task without abiding in you. I repent that I have tried

---

[40] Psalm 1:3 (KJV)
[41] John 15:5 (KJV)

to usurp your position by doing it all on my own. I choose, Lord, to relinquish all control to you so that I may be fruitful in all seasons. Lord, I ask that you make me a tree planted by the river. Lord, I ask that you deeply root me in your Word and confidence, and that though my branches sway in the storm, I will not be moved. Lord, I ask for the victory in my storms. Now, Lord, here I am, willing and able to do your will and be uprooted so you can replant me and make me deeply rooted. In Jesus's name, Amen.

Application

1. Imagine you abiding in Christ, taking all things to Him before you make a decision. What would that look like?

2. What fruit do you think you would bear if you continued to abide in Christ?

3. Think of one thing you have being doing in your own right and choose to give it to Christ.

4. Listen for His direction on that matter and be obedient to do as He says.

Make Notes Here:

Biblical Roots for Your Week

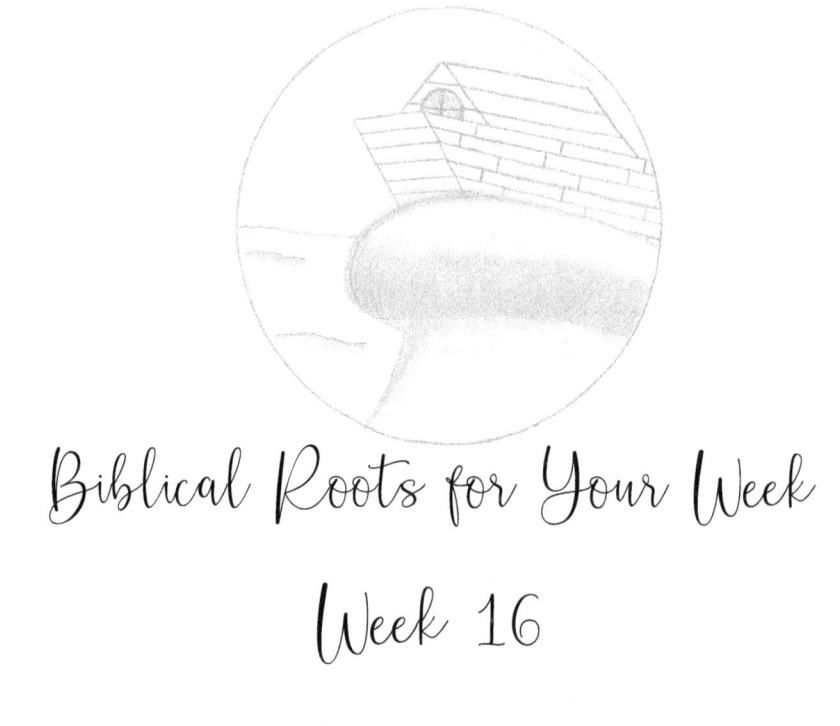

Week 16

Armored with faith, I hold the line for inevitable victories.

Armored for Battle

Have you ever heard someone say, "Hold the line"? It means to maintain your position. We have probably heard this in reference to the military, where military troops are taught to "hold the line" to prevent the enemy from breaking through.

We are all troops for the Lord tasked with "holding the line." We do not physically have to fight the enemy, but we are required to stand firm and hold our positions. 2 Chronicles 20:17 informs, "You will not have to fight this battle. [But you must] [t]ake up your positions; stand firm and see the deliverance the Lord will give you."

The reason we don't physically have to fight is because God has already won the war. Our salvation is intact, but the enemy is constantly working to steal, kill, and destroy. He has schemes to destroy us, our families, our marriages, our health, our careers, our friendships; the list is unending. Most importantly, he wants to destroy our faith.

The way we stand firm and hold our positions, or "hold the line," is by remaining faithful throughout all the enemy's schemes. Just as we put on our clothes every morning, we must be intentional in putting on "the whole armor of God, that [we] may be able to stand against the wiles of the devil."[42] The whole armor of God keeps us completely covered: the helmet of salvation, the breastplate of righteousness, the belt of truth, the feet for the gospel of peace, the shield of faith, and the sword of the spirit.[43]

If we are intentional to clothe ourselves every day with the whole armor of God, we can be confident we will "hold the line" against the wiles of the devil. We won't be afraid nor discouraged. We will be able to go out and face tomorrow.[44] Have you put on your armor today?

LaKeesha Griffin, God's pupil

Prayer

Lord, the Commander in Chief, I, (put your name here), thank you that you have clothed me with weapons of warfare to fight against the enemy. I thank you that I, because I am a soldier in your army, have the helmet of salvation, breastplate

---

[42] Ephesians 6:11
[43] Ephesians 6:14–17
[44] 2 Chronicles 20:17 (NIV)

of righteousness, belt of truth, feet for the gospel of peace, and sword of the Spirit to hold the line. Lord, I thank you that I am not charged with having to physically fight the enemy, nor will I ever have to, because you have already won the victory. Victory belongs to you, Father. And because you are victorious, I am, too. Lord, I repent that I have not been an active participant in holding the line. I repent that I have allowed the enemy to scare me into submission. I repent that I have often conceded to the enemy. I will do that no longer. Lord, I ask you to help me walk victoriously. I ask you to help me walk with my head held high and eyes on you. Lord, send me reminders that I should not fear the arrow by day or the terror by night. Now Lord, here I am, willing and able to do your will and hold the line. In Jesus's name, Amen.

Application

1. Write down the whole armor of God and place it where you normally get dressed every day.

2. Write down the most difficult situation you are currently facing.

3. How can you hold the line in that situation?

4. Pray specifically over that situation and ask God to give you the strength to hold the line.

Make Notes Here:

Biblical Roots for Your Week

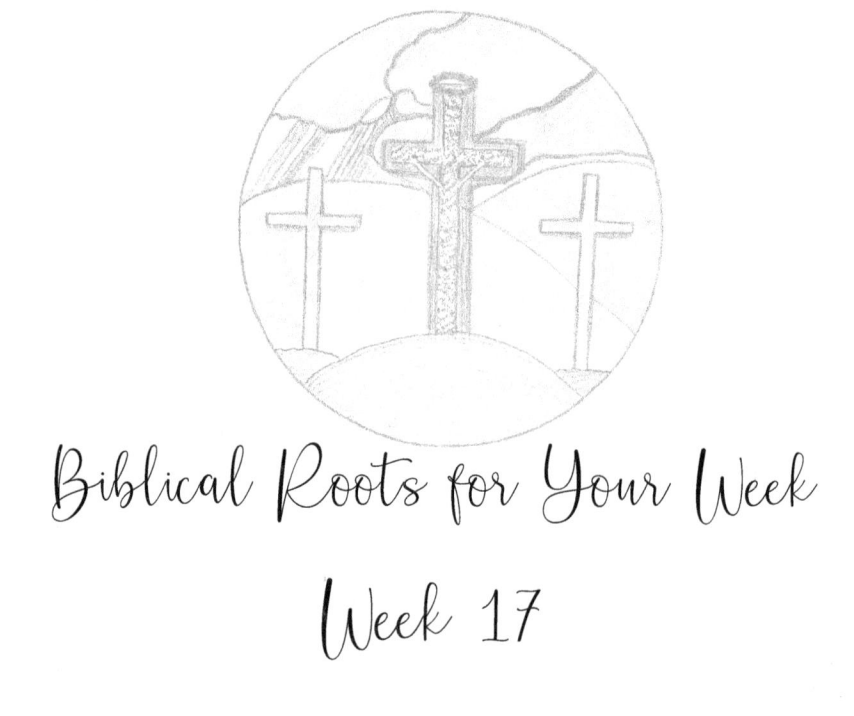

Week 17

Salvation is mine because Jesus placed no asterisks on substituting my place.

No Exception to the Rule

An "asterisk" (*) is used to give the reader, often within contractual terms, additional information. It is not only used to give additional information, but it is most often used to disclaim the referenced information or term. In this sense, it gives specific parameters for which the referenced information or term is or is not applicable; or to put it more simply, "asterisks" provide for exceptions.

With salvation, there are no "asterisks." When Jesus was asked by a Pharisee, "Teacher, which is the greatest commandment in the Law?" He put no "asterisks" on His response.[45] Jesus replied: "'Love the Lord your God with all your heart and with all your soul and with all your mind.' And the second is like it: 'Love your neighbor as yourself.'"[46] That is to say, Jesus commanded us to "love" Him and each other regardless. There are no disclaimers or parameters to that "love."

We are to "love" each other despite our discontent with each other, racial and socioeconomic differences, political affiliations, and so on. We are even to love those who have different beliefs and faiths. So, yes, that even means we "love" those who refuse to acknowledge our Lord and Savior, Jesus Christ.

What is so ironic is that the Pharisee, who was a strict observer of the traditional written Law, was the one asking Jesus this question. You see, the Pharisees were used to using "asterisks"; they didn't see that LOVE was more important when they questioned why Jesus would sit and dine with tax collectors and sinners.[47] Jesus warned them, saying, "Woe to you, teachers of the law and Pharisees, you hypocrites . . . [Y]ou have neglected the more important matters of the law."[48]

I encourage you to not neglect the more important matters of the law: LOVE! Only when we "love without an asterisk" are we obedient to those two prime commandments. No disclaimers! No parameters! Don't love with an asterisk!

LaKeesha Griffin, God's pupil

---

[45] Matthew 22:36 (NIV)
[46] Matthew 22:37–39 (NIV)
[47] (Matthew 9:11)
[48] Matthew 23:23 (NIV)

Prayer

Lord, you are Love, and I, (put your name here), thank you that because of your greatest example of love, I have a right to eternal life. God, thank you for choosing to send your only begotten son, Jesus, to die on the Cross for my sins so I may dwell with you eternally. Jesus, thank you for showing love beyond magnitude for me, someone so broken. Lord, I thank you that through my brokenness, your light shines. Lord, I repent that I have not loved without an asterisk. I repent that oftentimes what others do for me determines how I reciprocate love. Lord, I repent that I have not loved as you have commanded me to love. Lord, I choose to love as you love, without an asterisk. Lord, I ask you to help me love despite what others say or do against me. Help my love to reflect you so that others may see that love, glorify you, and love unconditionally in the same manner. Now Lord, here I am, willing and able to do your will and love without an asterisk. In Jesus's name, Amen.

Application

1. Who in your life you have loved with an asterisk?

2. Make a promise to God that you will love that person the way He has commanded you to love.

3. Make notes on how your newfound commitment to love that person without an asterisk affects how they reciprocate love to you.

4. Pray when you need strength to love that person beyond their faults.

Make Notes Here:

Biblical Roots for Your Week

Week 18

Fear is an emotional manifestation of the negative thoughts we choose to empower.

Fabricated Fear

If you have ever sat down and watched a horror movie, you know that everything you see is fabricated. However, as you get cozy under your blanket with some good popcorn, a good horror movie will draw you in. In an instant, though you're cognizant that it's a movie, it may still present in such a way that you forget this, and you'll allow it to scare you; in other words, within moments, we often forget it is a falsehood with the intention to scare us. That horror movie, like whatever you may fear right now, is "a fabricated sense of fear."

Fear is just like that; it is "a fabricated sense." The Word says in 2 Timothy 1:7 (KJV), "For God hath not given us the spirit of fear; but of power, and of love, and of a sound mind [or self-discipline]." So, who indeed gave us fear, or this "fabricated sense of fear"? Yes, you are exactly right: the enemy. It says it right there in the scripture; if it is not given by God, then it is given by the enemy. That scripture also tells us where the enemy works. It says he works in the spiritual world. In fact, the Word says in Ephesians 6:12 (KJV) that we wrestle/fight "against spiritual wickedness in high places." Thus, the enemy gives us fear or "a fabricated sense of fear" by working in the spiritual realm. This means we don't even see the fear being attached to us; he puts fear in us through a conning web of lies, broken-heartedness, failed relationships, and unhealthy decisions and environments. So, how do we fight against what we don't see?

The only way to fight against something in the spiritual world is by fighting against it with a spirit: the Holy Spirit! Tell the enemy to take his "fabricated sense of fear" and go to the place of horror he is condemned to for all eternity. The devil fears you when you are operating in the Spirit.

Never forget that the Holy Spirit has given you power, love, and a sound mind. No, no, no, devil, fear does not live here! Devil, go to Hell!!!!

LaKeesha Griffin, God's pupil

Prayer

Lord, you are one with the Holy Spirit; I, (put your name here), thank you that you have given me everything I need to walk through this valley of the shadow of death—power, love, and a sound mind. I thank you that you, too, operate in the spiritual realm, and that the enemy could never defeat you. Lord, you operate with power, love, and a sound mind. I thank you that you have given me what you, too, operate in to defeat the enemy in the spiritual realm. Lord, I have allowed the enemy to attach fear to me. I didn't even see it coming because he was so calculating in doing it. Lord, I repent for living in fear. I repent that fear has immobilized me, keeping me from my true purpose and the abundant life you have for me. I ask you, Father, to renew my mind and create a steadfast spirit with in me. I ask you, Holy Spirit, to work within me to fight against the spiritual wickedness that is coming at me from high places. Now Lord, here I am, willing and able to do your will and live to fight the enemy with the Holy Spirit. In Jesus's name, Amen.

Application

1. Write a list of all of your fears.

2. Be intentional to pray over each fear, saying this: Lord, I have been dealing with this (insert each fear here), but now, Holy Spirit, I ask you to give me power, love for myself, and self-discipline to defeat it. In Jesus's name, Amen.

3. Now, to see the physical manifestation of the fear disappearing, destroy the list (i.e., burn or shred it).

4. If you feel the fear being attached to you again, repeat the above steps.

Make Notes Here:

Biblical Roots for Your Week

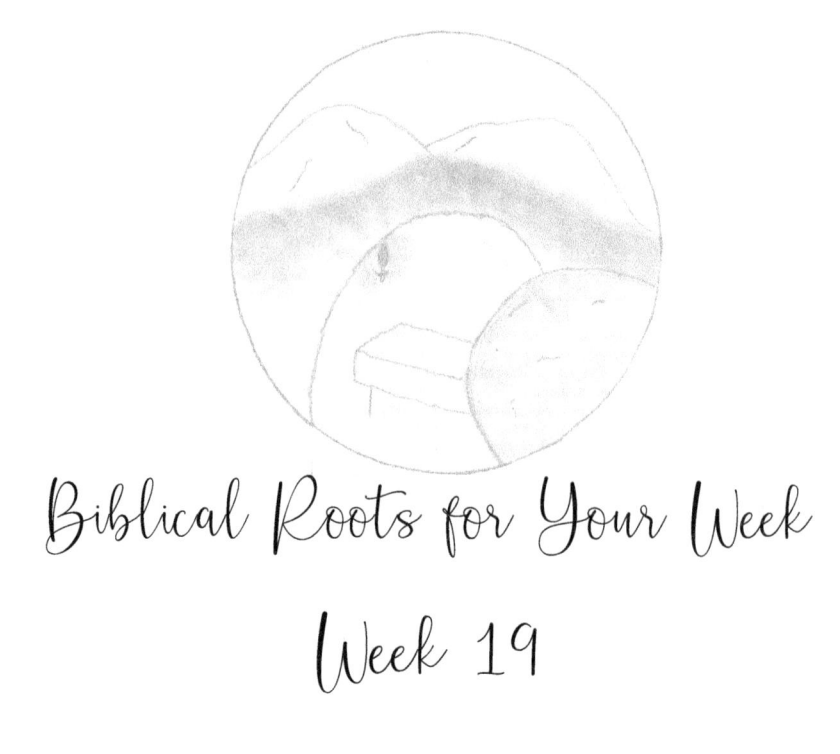

Week 19

To disassociate from those who make life unhealthy is an expression of self-care.

Reliable Friends?

Many of us have had the privilege of test driving a car. It is the dealership's attempt to wow us into a purchase. The ride may be smooth, and it checks all our boxes—it's the right size; it's the right look; and it's economical. However, have you ever had this experience: when you get it home and really put it to the test of the daily trials of your life (commuting, driving kids to school, vacation trip, etc.), you find it doesn't hold up to its value? You decide to redeem the warranty guarantee, but to no avail; your investment is a "lemon."

Some relationships are like this. No matter how you try to redeem the promises you were made, that person cannot and will never reflect your expectations. Why? Because you can't turn a "lemon" into orange juice. In this sense, it is more beneficial to take your "lemon" back and get something truly "reliable."

We have to know when God is leading us to disassociate ourselves from certain people so we may have someone in our lives who is more "reliable." Synonymously, when you find a good car, you can take it through the storms of life, and it will withstand. That car may have a lot of miles, dents, and rust, but it withstands. A true friend is like this—someone who helps you up when you fall down or is always there to pull you out of a pit.

In Ecclesiastes 4:10, the Word says to pity the one who is alone, because they have no one to help them when they fall. The Word is telling us that we cannot do life alone. I propose He is telling us that to do life, we need at least one "reliable" friend, who, despite the miles, dents, and rust, will continue to pray for us and with us—and, most importantly, will point us to Jesus, who ultimately "redeems [our lives] from the pit and crowns [us] with love and compassion."[49]

Jesus calls us His friends.[50] There's no truer friend than Him! But Jesus also wants us to have "reliable" friends to walk with us on our journey. I encourage you to evaluate your relationships and identify the "lemons." Who can you count on to pick you up when you fall down?

Stop trying to turn lemons into orange juice!

LaKeesha Griffin, God's pupil

---

[49] Psalm 103:4
[50] John 15:15

Prayer

Lord, my Very Best Friend, I, (put your name here), thank you that you call me friend. I thank you that because I am your friend, you reveal to me all things you have heard from your Father, God in Heaven. I thank you that you have chosen and ordained me to bear fruit. I acknowledge that it is by God's design that I have reliable friends in my life to hold me accountable in fulfilling my purpose for your Kingdom. Lord, I have not always chosen friends wisely. I have had friends to come and go, and in retrospect, I realize it is because I did not make their knowledge and belief in you a standard for how I chose them as a friend. Lord, I repent for allowing people in my friendship circle that only deterred me from my path to you and journey to my purpose. I ask you to help me evaluate my current friendship circle and give me the courage to sever ties with those who hinder me from bearing fruit. Now Lord, here I am, willing and able to do your will and have a friendship circle with reliable friends. In Jesus's name, Amen.

Application

1. Write a list of your current friends.

2. For each friend, write what they contribute to your spiritual growth.

3. For each friend, write what they contribute to your personal growth.

4. Make the decision to sever ties with the friends who are not contributing to both your spiritual and personal growth.

5. If there are any who contribute to both your spiritual and personal growth, charge them with being your accountability partner.

Make Notes Here:

Biblical Roots for Your Week

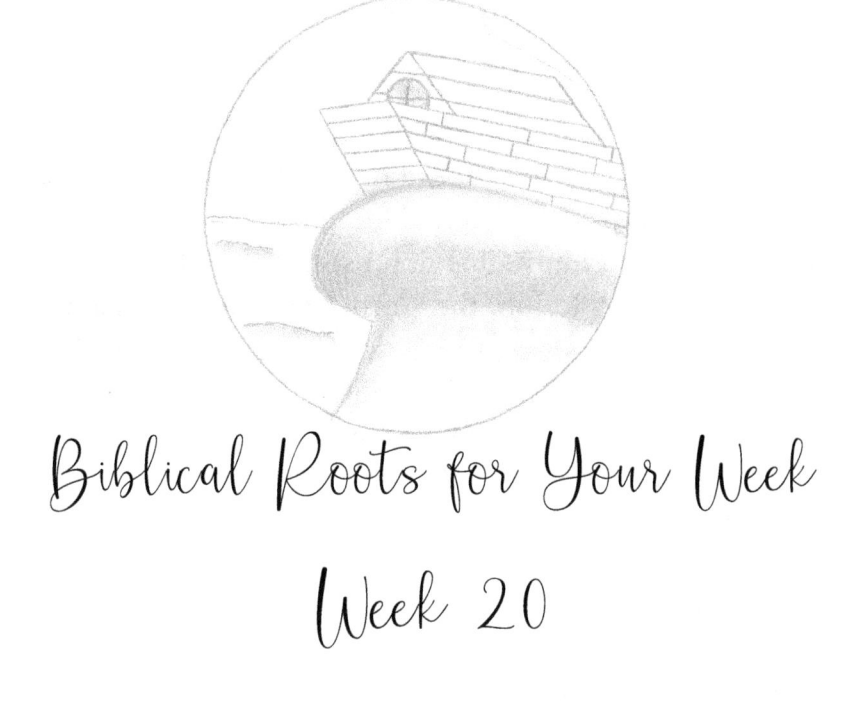

Week 20

Seeing the world through the lens of a child is the remedy to the world's brokenness.

Child-like Faith

Have you ever said that someone was operating in wisdom beyond their years? Perhaps you have said this: "You act like you've been here before!" Most likely, you were speaking to someone young or in reference to someone in their youth. Children often exhibit wisdom beyond our understanding.

Jesus thought highly of children. He said, "Let the children alone, and do not hinder them from coming to Me; for the kingdom of heaven belongs to such as these."[51] We gather

---
[51] Matthew 19:14 (NASB 1995)

from this scripture that children inherit the kingdom automatically. But why?

When talking to my son one day, he said, "I wish God was in this world!" He then spoke of not having to deal with bad health once he goes to be with Him. I explained to him that God is in this world; we just don't see Him, but we all have a cross to bear. I told him the Word says that we must deny ourselves, take up our cross, follow Him, and even be willing to lose our life to save it.[52] After telling my son that scripture, I explained it to him in the best way I thought a seven year old would understand: we all have a cross to bear, and if we do it willingly and still believe, it is an expression to God of our faith in Him. What better way to show our faith? How can faith be shown in any other way? You can't see the light without the darkness. You can't have a testimony without a test.

In hindsight, in that moment, I now know I was not looking at the world as my son was. I completely missed what he was saying because, as an adult, I was complicating the uncomplicated. Simply put, my son was saying, the world needs Jesus! Children can see the world differently from us because their view is untainted and uncorrupted by sin. This is why Jesus can automatically give the kingdom of heaven to a child; they see the world for what it truly is—a world in need of Jesus!

If we can seek out having a "child-like" faith like this, we will see every one of our situations as it truly is; that is, that we need Jesus for the world's (our) brokenness. If we look at everything in our lives as a child does, then eternity in heaven is automatic: "Truly I tell you, unless you CHANGE

---

[52] Luke 9:23–24

and become like little children, you will never enter the kingdom of heaven."[53]

LaKeesha Griffin, God's pupil

Prayer

Lord, my Father, I, (put your name here), thank you that you call me your child. I thank you that because I am your child, I have inherited the Kingdom of Heaven. I thank you that as long as I love as a child of yours should, I will receive the Kingdom of Heaven automatically. You said to not hinder your children from coming to you. I thank you that there is no hindrance or barrier that I must face to get to you. I know this gift of being free to come to you is the gift I inherited when you died on the Cross for my sins. Thank you, Father. Lord, I repent that I complicate the uncomplicated. I repent that I have been unable to see the world like a child sees it. I know, Lord, that I can only change with your help. I ask you now to help me change and see the world as a child of yours should. Now Lord, here I am, willing and able to do your will and allow you to change me to become like a child. In Jesus's name, Amen.

Application

1. Do your best to embody the thinking of a child, then simplify what you think is wrong with the world.

---

[53] Matthew 18:3 (NIV)

2. How can you be instrumental in influencing others to see things more simply? Make a commitment to doing so.

3. Think about one obstacle you may be facing (i.e., a rude boss, wayward child, or an estranged spouse) and write down a child-like antidote for the obstacle.

4. Ask Jesus to cure the situation you are facing, then commit to seeing the situation as a child does.

Make Notes Here:

Biblical Roots for Your Week

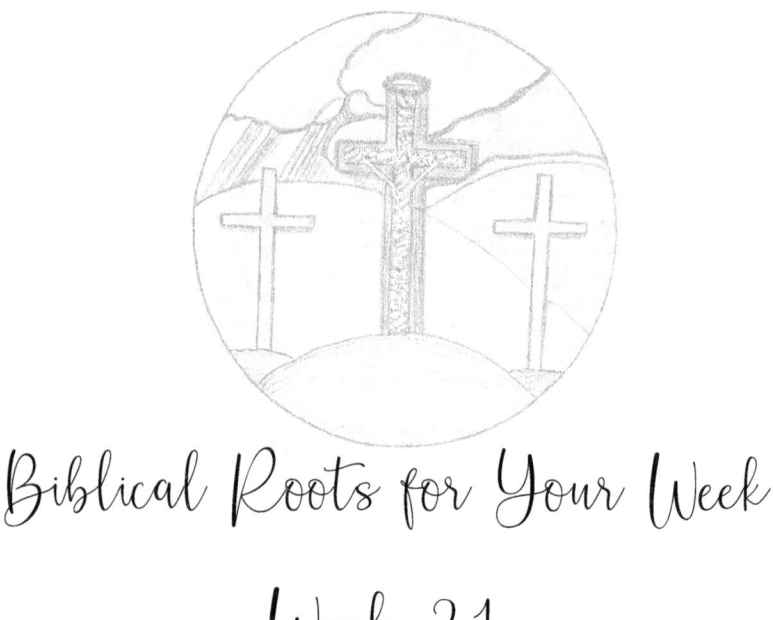

Week 21

When one sees temptation as only a challenge to overcome, they reach the other side of victory.

Tempted but Fortified

Being tempted by the devil "fortifies" our souls. I know that sounds completely ridiculous, but it's the truth: when we are tempted by the devil, our souls are strengthened, but *only* if we respond with the Word of God. Sometimes we are led by the Spirit to be challenged or tempted by the devil. To be "challenged" is to threaten someone's claim to something. The devil challenges us by threatening our claim of salvation, a renewed mind, and reformed life. Even Jesus was challenged: the Spirit led Jesus to be challenged by the devil in the wilderness.[54] How did Jesus respond to the challenge? Jesus responded with the Word of God.

The devil took Jesus to two different places; the devil took Jesus to the holy city and to a high mountain in an attempt to lead Him astray. But Jesus *only* responded with the Word of God.[55] Sometimes the devil throws obstacles in our way in an attempt to lead us astray. He thinks we are in that place by his doing; He thinks the obstacles he has contrived will be our undoing. However, the devil is unaware that we are in front of that obstacle not because he led us there, but because the Holy Spirit has allowed us to be there to "fortify" our souls. You see, the Holy Spirit is aware of what we need to get to the point where we respond with *only* the Word of God. In other words, the Holy Spirit knows the formula for us to reach only God. When Jesus was tempted those three times in the wilderness by the devil, He responded, "Just God"; consequently, the devil had no other choice than to leave, then "angels came and attended to [Jesus]."[56]

Don't give the devil the glory to think he has you where he wants you; tell him you are here by design, and that on the other side of victory, the angels are waiting to attend to you. "Resist the devil, and he will flee from you."[57] How do you resist? "Just God!"

LaKeesha Griffin, God's pupil

---

[54] Matthew 4:1
[55] Matthew 4:5–10
[56] Matthew 4:11 (NIV)
[57] James 4:7 (NIV)

Prayer

Lord, the Overcomer, I, (put your name here), thank you that you have overcome the enemy despite all his tricks to tempt you. I thank you that you fulfilled your purpose to overcome the enemy by only using the Word of God. I believe the Word of God is the most powerful weapon to overcome the enemy; it is living and active. It is sharper than any two-edged sword and has the power to penetrate the deepest parts of man. I thank you that the Word of God has penetrated my soul. I repent that I have not responded to my obstacles with only the Word of God. Lord, I repent that I have often responded to the world as the world expects me to. Now, Lord, I ask you to give me the strength to respond with only the Word of God. Please, Father, give me a "Just God" approach to all things in my life. Now Lord, here I am, willing and able to do your will and respond to all temptation with the Word of God. In Jesus's name, Amen.

Application

1. Be truthful with yourself and write down what you think your greatest temptation is.

2. Repent that you have fallen victim to that temptation, and ask for forgiveness.

3. Find a scripture that you will use from now on to respond to the enemy when he tempts you with that temptation.

4. Repeat the above steps for any temptation you find yourself falling victim to frequently.

5. Continue to ask God for overcoming strength.

Make Notes Here:

Biblical Roots for Your Week

Week 22

An open coffer gives God permission to revive what seems dead.

Being Open to Restoration

A "coffin" is a box in which a dead loved one is buried. A "coffer" is fairly related to the term "coffin." Like a "coffin" used to keep our deceased loved one in, a "coffer" is also a strong box in which we can keep valuables.

In Luke 7:11–15, Jesus and the disciples went into a city, and near a gate, a dead man was being carried out in his coffin. The mother of the man was weeping nearby; this woman had no one left in her family. She was a widow, and the dead man in the coffin was her only son. Jesus looked upon her and had compassion. He reached out and touched the "open coffin"; Jesus said, "Young man, I say to you, arise."[58] You already know what happened next. After all, we are talking about Jesus. He sure did; that young man got up![59]

Some of us have "dead coffers." In other words, what we would normally keep in our "coffers" is dead. For example, your finances may be dead. But Jesus sees you weeping from the lack in your life, and He looks on you with compassion. Jesus always has compassion for the things that are dead in our lives. He wants to bring what we value back to life—our joy, peace, hope, health, family, finances, and so on.

I encourage you to lift your "coffers" up to Jesus, and like the weeping woman who got back what she valued, Jesus will restore back to you what you value. However, the key to Jesus restoring what you value is whether you have your "coffer" *open* to Him. He won't bless a closed "coffer." He can't bless what you won't *open* up to Him.

What's in your "coffer?" Is it dead? *Open* it up and let Jesus touch it!!!

LaKeesha Griffin, God's Pupil

Prayer

Lord, the Resurrector, I, (put your name here), thank you that you restore unto me all things I have lost. I thank you that because of you, I am confident that my latter will be greater than my former. I thank you that you have compassion on me when I have lost what is valuable to me. I thank you

---

[58] Luke 7:14 (NKJV)
[59] Luke 7:15

that your compassion compels you to reach out and resurrect what is dead in my life. Lord, there are things that are dead in my life that I wish were revived. I have carried those things around in a closed coffer instead of an open one. Lord, I repent that my coffer has not been open to you. I open my coffer now, and with everything I consider valuable inside, I give it to you to resurrect. I ask you to help me to continue to walk in faith as I await the revival of the things I thought I lost. Give me patience, Father, and a peace that surpasses my own understanding. Now Lord, here I am, willing and able to do your will and open my coffer to you. In Jesus's name, Amen.

Application

1. Write a list of things you consider valuable (i.e., your dreams, a business idea, marriage, etc.).

2. Make an evaluation on whether those things need restoration.

3. For each thing, ask God to restore unto you those things you have lost.

4. Hand each thing over to God in an open coffer by saying this for each thing you value: Lord, I give you (insert each thing you value here) to resurrect from the dead.

5. Trust that God has compassion for you and will resurrect what you value.

Make Notes Here:

Biblical Roots for Your Week

Week 23

Having hands up and heart humble is a posture of surrender before winning the battle.

Surrender to Win

We have all seen when, in the midst of a battle, one side surrenders. When we think of someone "surrendering" in a battle, we most often think they have their "hands up." In this world, having our "hands up" in the midst of a battle means we are ceasing resistance of the enemy; in other words, we acknowledge defeat.

In Exodus 17:8–13, the Amalekites came and attacked the Israelites. Moses instructed Joshua to choose some men to fight against the Amalekites. What was Moses doing during this time? Instead of fighting, he was "surrendering." No, he did not "surrender" to the Amalekites. The Word tells us that Moses stood atop the hill with the staff of God in his "hands."[60] Indeed, amid the battle, Moses was "surrendering" to God. It was a long battle, but as long as Moses's *hands were lifted up*, the Israelites were winning; and whenever he lowered his hands, the Amalekites were winning.[61] Cognizant of the power of "surrendering" in the middle of a battle, as Moses's hands grew tired, Aaron and Hur first took a stone to *prop Moses's hands up,* and then finally, with one on each side, they *held Moses' hands up*.[62] What was the result? Victory!!!

God wants us to "surrender" in the midst of our battles. As long as we have our "hands lifted up," we win! This way of fighting a battle provides a guaranteed win. This scriptural lesson teaches us that we need to *surrender to God* to be victorious, but also, when we grow tired, we need other people (accountability partners) to help. We need other people in our fight against the enemy to help us keep our "hands up" in "surrender."

I encourage you to rethink having your "hands up" in a battle as a sign that you are ceasing resistance of the enemy; instead, think, "If I have my 'hands up' in this battle, that is because I am submitting to the ultimate authority. I am guaranteed to win!" Get someone to help you in your fight to keep your "hands lifted up!" Lifted hands yield a victory! Lowered hands yield defeat!

LaKeesha Griffin, God's Pupil

---

[60] Exodus 17:9
[61] Exodus 17:12
[62] Exodus 17:12

Prayer

Lord, you are Mighty in Battle; I, (put your name here), thank you that you are all-powerful, always present, and all-knowing. Because you are indeed omnipotent, omnipresent, and omniscient, you are prepared to win every attack from the enemy. You are my victory banner, Father. You reign supreme. I see my surrender to you as a sign of strength, not weakness. Because I surrender to you, I am guaranteed an automatic win. Lord, I repent that I have not gone into battle with my hands lifted up in surrender to you. I repent that I have not gone into battle with others who are willing to prop my hands up in surrender to you. Lord, I ask you to keep me cognizant of your power. Keep me in a posture of surrender. Lord, I also ask that you show me those who are willing to go into battle with me in a posture of surrender. Lord, I surrender to you now and forever. Now Lord, here I am, willing and able to do your will and surrender in perpetuity. In Jesus's name, Amen.

Application

1. What current battle(s) are you facing that you have not surrendered to God?

2. Identify God-fearing accountability partners that you have around you.

3. Designate the battle(s) you face to a respective accountability partner.

4. Be mindful to contact that accountability partner any time you feel you are not in a posture of surrender to God regarding the battle.

Make Notes Here:

Biblical Roots for Your Week

Week 24

To learn the Word of God is to keep it stored in your heart for the offensive attack against the defense.

Learned Faith

What's your "learning" style? Is your "learning" style visual, auditory, reading/writing, or kinesthetic (meaning you learn by doing)? There is no right or wrong way by which we can "learn" something. What's important is that we "learn" it.

God says, "*Study* to show thyself approved unto God, a workman that needeth not to be ashamed, rightly dividing the word of truth."[63] God knows that only by *studying* can

---

[63] 2 Timothy 2:15 (KJV)

we hide the word in our hearts so that we do not sin against Him.[64] In other words, we can only apply to our lives what we have "learned."

Scripture doesn't specify one way for "learning" God's Word or principles for Godly living; in fact, God knows that the only way some of us can "learn" is by visualizing, listening, reading/writing, or doing. God, in His infinite wisdom, has us (every "learning" style) covered. For the *visual learner*, set your minds on things above, not on the things of the earth.[65] This is what I call having a heavenly mindset. For the *auditory learner*, He has graced you with sermons via the internet, church, and even Bible apps that will read you the Word via audio. God knows "faith cometh by hearing, and hearing by the Word of God."[66] "The wise will hear and increase their learning."[67] For the one who "learns" via *reading or writing*, the Bible is rich in scripture for life applications; when you read and write the Word in different places, you are allowing God to write on your heart. How are you allowing God to write on your heart by reading His word? You are allowing Him to breathe it into you: "every part of scripture is God-breathed and useful one way or another—showing us truth, exposing our rebellion, correcting our mistakes, training us to live God's way."[68] Lastly, for the *kinesthetic learner*, who learns by doing, God definitely has you covered. He allows all of us to "learn" from our mistakes, failures, and temptations. God knows that when we

---

[64] Psalm 119:11
[65] Colossians 3:2 (NKJV)
[66] Romans 10:17 (KJV)
[67] Proverbs 1:5 (AMP)
[68] 2 Timothy 3:14:17 (MSG)

face trials of many kinds, "the testing of [our] faith produces perseverance."[69]

Whatever your "learning" style, God has you covered. He promises that He will be faithful to complete the good work He started in you.[70] He will make sure you "learn" what is necessary to become the best you, even if He has to teach it to you (or you have to "learn" it) several times.

LaKeesha Griffin, God's pupil

Prayer

Lord, you are All-knowing; I, (put your name here), thank you that you, in your infinite wisdom, made provision for me to learn your Word in a way that allows me to chew on it and digest it so that it bears fruit in my heart. Lord, I thank you that I, too, have the opportunity to become wise if I study your Word. I know that only by studying your Word will I be able to hide it in my heart. Thank you, Lord, for the many ways and mediums through which I am able to learn your Word. Lord, I repent that I have not studied your Word well enough for it to be deeply rooted in my heart. I repent that I need to find more time to get personally acquainted with your Word. Lord, I acknowledge that I can only receive power by your Word. Lord, help me to find more time to study and learn your Word. Now Lord, here I am, willing and able to do your will and hide your Word in my heart. In Jesus's name, Amen.

---

[69] James 1:2–4 (NIV)
[70] Philippians 1:6

Application

1. What do you think is your learning style(s)?
2. Why do you think this is your learning style(s)?
3. How can you apply that learning style to studying and hiding the Word in your heart?
4. Make a plan to use your learning style to get personally acquainted with the Word of God.

Make Notes Here:

Biblical Roots for Your Week

Week 25

To be counted as sheep is to carry on the legacy of Christ.

True Legacy

What would you like your "legacy" to be? Fame, fortune, popularity, skill, talent, athleticism, Grammy or Oscar Awards, your name in lights? I, myself, choose a "legacy" that will translate into eternal living—to feed the hungry, to give drink to the thirsty, to invite the stranger in, to provide clothes to those who don't have them, to tend to the sick, and to visit the imprisoned.[71] This is the "legacy" God has chosen for all of us, because all the other stuff doesn't matter. In fact, God distinguishes those who do this as His

---

[71] Matthew 25:34–36

"sheep" and those who do not as "goats." And as King, He says He will separate the "sheep" from the "goats."[72] He will say to His "sheep," "Whatever you did for one of the least of these brothers and sisters of mine, you did for me."[73] To the "goats"—those who are just making vain attempts at self-gratification rather than servanthood—He will say that if you did not do it to the least of them, you did not do it unto Him.[74] He promises that the "sheep" will go on to eternal life, and the "goats" will go on to eternal punishment.[75]

There was a rich man who claimed he had done everything right, but when Jesus told him to sell all his possessions and give the money to the poor to gain eternal life, the man refused.[76] That man cared more about his "legacy" as a rich man. Riches or vanity don't translate to eternal living. So, what in this world translates to eternal living? The answer is simple: when we do for God by doing for others. This is the "legacy" we should choose because it is the only thing on Earth that will manifest in Heaven. He will then say, "Hey, (insert your name here), I know you well because you did for me when you did for others. You are my sheep." Then He will say, "Well done, my good and faithful servant. You have been faithful because you (insert what you did unto the least of them here), so come on in, (insert your name here)."[77] This gives new meaning to saying that only what you do for Christ will last.[78]

---

[72] Matthew 25:33
[73] Matthew 25:40 (NIV)
[74] Matthew 25:46
[75] Matthew 25:46
[76] Matthew 19:16–22
[77] Matthew 25:21
[78] 1 John 2:17

When you depart from this world, wouldn't you rather hear that you were a faithful servant and see Heaven's door open unto you, instead of Jesus turning from you and saying nothing at all because He doesn't know you? Make your "legacy" His will for your life. Are you His "sheep" or the world's "goat?"

LaKeesha Griffin, God's pupil

Prayer

Lord, my Shepherd, I, (put your name here), thank you that as a shepherd, you tend to your flock. I thank you that you call your sheep by name, and because you know me by name, that means you know everything about me. I thank you that because I am your sheep, you keep the wolves from pursuing me. Father, I commit to living a life that has an eternal impact. I will do unto the least of my brothers and sisters because I want to make sure I am doing all good things unto you. Lord, I repent that I have pursued a legacy that only the world values. Lord, I repent that I have rationalized when I should bless others. You said to just to do it, so now, Lord, I commit to blessing others regardless. I ask that you keep me in a posture to give instead of receiving. Thank you for showing me what a heavenly legacy should look like. Now Lord, here I am, willing and able to do your will and do unto the least of my brothers and sisters. In Jesus's name, Amen.

Application

1. Be honest with yourself and write what you would like your legacy to be once you depart from this world.

2. Evaluate whether your intended legacy is a heavenly legacy—that is, whether it reflects giving to other unfortunate brothers and/or sisters.

3. If it does not reflect a heavenly legacy, then write your intended legacy in a way that includes providing for other less fortunate brothers and/or sisters.

4. Consider joining a ministry whose purpose is to give unto the less fortunate (i.e., the homeless ministry, prison ministry, feeding the elderly, etc.).

Make Notes Here:

Biblical Roots for Your Week

Week 26

Only the one who creates holds the manual to fix His creation.

Lingering Brokenness?

Have you ever cleaned behind someone who broke something fragile, like a mirror, porcelain plate, or glass cup? If so, you know to proceed with caution and not to walk around without any shoes. You immediately sweep up what is broken. But maybe later, even a couple of days later, you are walking around, and you step on a remaining broken piece.

    Sometimes in life, we try to clean up somebody else's brokenness. We think we have done well because, on the surface, things seem to be going well. But then reality hits; we then find out that they have a remaining broken piece. In other words, their "brokenness has been left behind."

The Word of God points to us as clay and to God as the potter.[79] Just like with any creator or manufacturer of something, only God knows how to mend the brokenness of His creation. He shines His illuminating light on all the heartache, pain, despair, isolation, and any and everything that has caused our brokenness so that we can personally identify it and not hide it in a corner to be revealed later, like the broken piece of glass on the floor. Then, He alone works to put us back together. Now, when we return to a semblance of what we used to be, His light radiates from the cracks where we were once broken. Then, we finally get to see the beauty in our brokenness.

Only God can illuminate the brokenness, put the broken back together, and make the broken whole. Stop trying to fix other people! Haven't you seen that in your human attempts to do so, there is "brokenness left behind?"

Let God fix His creation. We are all the work of His hand![80]

LaKeesha Griffin, God's pupil

Prayer

Lord, the Potter, I, (put your name here), thank you that you created me. I thank you that your creation is marvelous, and that you know it well. I thank you that you mend me back together when I am broken. I thank you that you don't stop there. You then go on to let your light shine through

---

[79] Isaiah 64:8
[80] Isaiah 64:8

my brokenness. Lord, I realize that only you can fix the brokenness in my life. I also realize that only you can fix the brokenness in other's lives. Lord, I repent that I have both tried to fix my own brokenness and the brokenness of others. Forgive me, Father, for attempting to do only what you can do, which is to make all things new. Lord, I ask that you make me new. Mend my brokenness, Father. I am living a façade that I am whole, but truly, Lord, I am broken and need your healing touch. Now Lord, here I am, willing and able to do your will and allow you to put me back together so I can see the beauty in my brokenness. In Jesus's name, Amen.

Application

1. What is broken in your life?

2. How have you tried, in your own might, to fix the brokenness in your life?

3. Have you tried, in your own might, to fix the brokenness in someone else's life (i.e., a spouse, child, family member, or friend)?

4. Make a commitment to release yourself from the inevitable failure of trying to fix yourself or someone else and allow God to do His job as Potter.

Make Notes Here:

Biblical Roots for Your Week

Week 27

If I limit the greatness living on the inside of me, I will never reach my destiny.

Internal Greatness

"Greatness" is living on the inside of you, but it has nothing to do with you—not your educational attainments, career title, estate value, associations, stature, genes, or even family legacy. "Greatness" is in you because God dwells in you. Even if you disagree that something great is happening in your life right now, it doesn't negate the "greatness" within you.

"You, dear children, are from God, and have overcome them, because the one who is in you is greater than the one who is in the world."[81] This is something you learned back in elementary—that is, comparing and contrasting values, like what is greater than, less than, or equal to. Let's take that analysis: the version of yourself operating in this world is operating with limited power because you are operating in only your human abilities. Thus, when you are operating, you are the one in control of your life, and so your "greatness" is suppressed. However, when you are not operating or not wielding control and instead being totally submissive to God, God is operating. It is no surprise that when God is operating, your power is limitless. When God's power has no restraints, greater is He who is in you than you who are in the world. 1 John 4:4. This is when you are empowered by His "greatness."

Naturally, this question follows: are you operating? I hope not, but if so, I encourage you to give up your limited control and power to the all-powerful God, the one and only who controls your "right now" and your destiny. It is when He is in control that He perfects that which concerns you.[82]

As long as you're in your own way, your attempts at joy, happiness, and true purpose will always be a less than attempt at what our Great God can do with His "greatness." Why? Because "greatness" is equal to God.

LaKeesha Griffin, God's pupil

Prayer

Lord, my Greatness, I, (put your name here), thank you that you dwell within me. Because you dwell within me, greatness

---

[81] 1 John 4:4 (NIV)
[82] Psalm 138:8 (KJV)

can manifest in my life. I acknowledge that all I have to do to experience that manifestation is to yield to your greatness. Lord, I yield to your greatness and give you complete control so that the power I operate in is limitless. I thank you for perfecting those things which concern me. I thank you that there is nothing that compares to your power. Lord, I repent that I have been operating in my own human abilities. I repent that I have placed restraints on how and when you can operate in my life. I ask you to empower me, Father, with your greatness. Now Lord, here I am, willing and able to do your will and yield to your absolute control and power in my life. In Jesus's name, Amen.

Application

1. What are some things you have been trying to accomplish in your own abilities (i.e., business launching, financial security, etc.)?

2. Have you asked God to take control of them? If you have, have you trusted that He will do it?

3. If the things you are hoping for seem daunting, write down a scripture that reflects God's power regarding that thing.

4. Every time you feel yourself taking back control from God, repent, then remind yourself of that scripture.

Make Notes Here:

Biblical Roots for Your Week

Week 28

I count it great joy that the devil is jealous of me.

A Friend of Christ

Jealously is never looked upon as a good character trait. But God Himself explains that He is a jealous God; we should not bow or submit ourselves to anyone but Him.[83] I learned from a marital conference that God being a jealous God is likened to the jealousy a spouse feels when someone outside of that covenant relationship threatens the marriage; like God being jealous, if someone within the marital confines gives their heart to someone or something else, jealously is valid. At the conference, we were taught that this is called

---

[83] Exodus 20:2–6

"legitimate jealously."[84] I propose to you that there is another example of "legitimate jealously" that we never think about and will explain what we may be currently facing in our lives.

The devil is "legitimately jealous" of you!!! Don't believe me? John 12:9–11 explains how the chief priests planned to kill Lazarus, whom Jesus had raised from the dead, because via that act, more people began to believe in Him. It is no clearer than that: the enemy plots to kill you because of your friendship with Jesus!!! The enemy does this because he is "legitimately jealous" of you.

The devil knows firsthand what Heaven with Jesus feels like. He knows it was his worst mistake that by his actions, he fell from Heaven into Hell[85] and lost his position of authority, leaving his God-provided dwelling only to be kept in everlasting chains.[86] His sentence of restraint is forever. Meanwhile, he sees that your obedience to God elevates you from which he came. He doesn't want you to walk in obedience, in love for others, and definitely not in freedom. He hates that Jesus considers you His friend, and because of this friendship, whatever you ask in Jesus's name, the Father will give you.[87]

Your friendship with Jesus gives you great power and authority—the power and authority that the devil had, but lost. It's that same power and authority that you now use to trample upon snakes and scorpions—or the devil—stripping the enemy from all semblance of what it felt like to be God's friend.[88]

---

[84] Evans, Jimmy. *The Four Laws of Love* (2019)
[85] Isaiah 14:12–15
[86] Jude 1:6 (NIV)
[87] John 15:15–16
[88] Luke 10:19

When considering a broken friendship, the one who broke up the friendship will do their very best to isolate that old friend from other people. The devil is no different. So, when the enemy is being disruptive in your life, count it all joy.[89]

The devil has every reason, by his own doing, to be "legitimately jealous" of you. He is no longer Christ's friend, but you are!!!

LaKeesha Griffin, God's pupil

Prayer

Lord, my Only True Friend, I, (put your name here), thank you that you love me so much that you would want to be my friend. I thank you that the enemy could never sever our relationship as friends. I thank you that because I am your friend, you extend to me the power and authority to trample on snakes and scorpions. I acknowledge that I have the authority to put the devil back in his earned place, Hell. Thank you for the power I graciously get because I am your friend. Lord, I repent that I have not used my friendship card to send the enemy back to Hell. I repent that I have seen the enemy as too powerful to fight back. I ask you, Father, to renew my mind regarding my relationship with you. Help me to see the value of our friendship. Now Lord, here I am, willing and able to do your will and use my friendship card you've given me. In Jesus's name, Amen.

---

[89] James 1:2 (KJV)

Application

1. In your opinion, what is the true nature of friendship?

2. Does God meet that definition for you? Why or why not?

3. Write down scripture that directly reflects your definition of true friendship as it relates to God.

4. Choose to see God as your true friend.

Make Notes Here:

Biblical Roots for Your Week

Week 29

The key to becoming a vessel of honor is permitting the Holy Spirit to dwell within you.

Being a Spiritual Host

On *America's Got Talent*, there, to showcase her talent, was a little girl. The backstory was that her mother encouraged this talent to give her something to look forward to and increase her social interaction because she was being bullied at school. This talent, one we have all seen before, was ventriloquism. This is when a person creates the illusion that a puppet is speaking by immersing themselves within the puppet. However, it appears that the person, who is actually speaking, is uninvolved in the process. Let's look at it in a different way.

In science, we learn about the concept of a host. It is when another organism lives and thrives in another. Synonymously, the puppet is a host because the little girl immerses herself into the puppet, lives there, and thrives there. Accordingly, the puppet is a vessel in which the little girl manifests her true God-intended self.

We are called to be vessels of honor—to be "sanctified, and *meet* for the master's use, and prepared unto every good work,"[90] The only way we become a vessel of honor is by purging ourselves from that which is dishonorable.[91] That means to be a vessel of honor, we must act with honor, which means following after "righteousness, faith, charity, peace . . . call[ing] on the Lord out of a pure heart"[92] and "be[ing] gentle unto all men, apt to teach, patient, [and] in meekness instructing those that oppose themselves."[93] On the opposite coin, this means that we must evade the works of the flesh."[94] The only way we can do this is by allowing ourselves to be a host. If we allow ourselves to be a host for the Holy Spirit to dwell within us, we manifest the fruits of the Spirit: "love, joy, peace, longsuffering, gentleness, goodness, faith, meekness, temperance."[95]

Now, go back to the initial scripture, 2 Timothy 2:21. In that scripture is the word *meet*. Meet means to touch or join. If we allow ourselves to be a host unto the Spirit (or we allow the Spirit to touch or join within us), then we are automatically a vessel of honor because to "live in the Spirit . . . [is to]

---

[90] 2 Timothy 2:21 (KJV)
[91] 2 Timothy 2:21 (KJV)
[92] 2 Timothy 2:22 (KJV)
[93] 2 Timothy 2:24–25 (KJV)
[94] Galatians 5:19 (KJV)
[95] Galatians 5:22–23 (KJV)

walk in the Spirit."[96] Consequently, by becoming a vessel of honor, God is manifesting our true God-intended self.

LaKeesha Griffin, God's pupil

Prayer

Lord, you are one with the Spirit; I, (put your name here), thank you that you live in me and are directly responsible for me bearing the fruits of the Spirit. I thank you that because I am a willing vessel, you are making me a vessel of honor. I know that produces a manifestation of who you have called me to truly be. I thank you that I will soon be my true God-intended self. Lord, I repent that I have not evaded the fruits of the flesh when I should have. Lord, I know you intend for me to live and walk in the Spirit. But I admit and now repent that I have not done so. I ask for your forgiveness, Father. I ask you to live within me as your vessel. I ask you to help me live day-to-day bearing the fruits of the Spirit. Help me to love despite the faults of others. Help me to keep joy stored in my heart. Give me a peace which surpasses my understanding. Help me to persevere through trials despite the forecasted outcome or prognosis. Help me to be gentle and always good to others. Give me faith that mountains will be removed. Help me to walk with humility, and help me to practice self-restraint. Now Lord, here I am, willing and able to do your will and live as a vessel unto your Spirit. In Jesus's name, Amen.

Application

1. Write down the fruits of the Spirit.

---

[96] Galatians 5:25 (KJV)

2. Write down what you think each fruit of the Spirit means.

3. Now, write down an example of when you reflected each fruit of the Spirit.

4. Resolve within yourself that you are not perfect, that you make mistakes, and that you can always repent, receive forgiveness, and continue to live and walk in the Spirit.

Make Notes Here:

Biblical Roots for Your Week

Week 30

The Light of the world exposes all that lurks in the shadows.

Deep Cleansing

Have you ever paid to have your car detailed? After it is detailed, it looks brand new, like it was when you purchased it from the dealership. You get in it, and it is freshly scented. However, upon "deeper" evaluation, you find food remnants and trash from your daily routine still in the crevices and creases. Now, how could you have paid for a "deep cleaning" and not received it? The answer is this: only what was visible was cleaned. Man doesn't know how to "deeply clean" the trash in our lives. We on our own might try to do it; we parade around as if everything is hunky-dory, putting on the façade that we are okay, but, truthfully, we can't even "deeply clean" our own lives.

Only God knows when we need a "deep cleaning" and in what areas to shine His light to reveal the trash in our lives. Jesus makes us holy by cleansing us and washing us with water through the Word so that He may present us in Heaven without stain, wrinkle, or blemish; instead, we appear holy and blameless.[97] God, as the Light, goes to the creases and crevices, or the depths of our soul, and *deeply cleanses* us from all unrighteousness. He makes "his light shine in our hearts to give us the light of the knowledge of God's glory displayed in the face of Christ."[98]

What does the "deep cleaning" yield? It yields a new mind; He gives us the mind of Christ.[99] Now, instead of cussing out the one who cut you off in traffic, you pray for their safety. He turns our heart of stone to flesh and gives us a new spirit.[100] Now, instead of your boss or co-worker getting on your nerves, you see their human condition, sympathize, and testify to them of the goodness of the Lord.

God washes us whiter than snow.[101] He "deeply cleans" us from the inside out. Brand spanking new! No remnants left in the crevices or creases. His light exposes it all. And guess what? We didn't even have to pay for it. Jesus paid for it all!

LaKeesha Griffin, God's pupil

---

[97] Ephesians 5:25–27 (NIV)
[98] 2 Corinthians 4:6 (NIV)
[99] 1 Corinthians 2:16
[100] Ezekiel 36:26–27
[101] Isaiah 1:18

Prayer

Lord, the Deep Cleanser, I, (put your name here), thank you that there is no part of me you don't see. Everything I hide from man, Lord, you are able to shine your light on, not to shame me, but to bring me healing. I thank you that you have cleansed me from all unrighteousness. Lord, I know that although I am not perfect, with you I walk on the righteous path. One day, I know I will be presented before you without a stain, wrinkle, or blemish because of the work you have done in me. Lord, I repent that I walk around pretending everything is okay instead of calling out to you for help. Lord, I repent of the trash remaining in the creases and crevices that I have tried to keep hidden. I ask you, Father, to expose it all. Please shine your light on those areas in my life that you need to deeply cleanse. Now Lord, here I am, willing and able to do your will and let your light shine on my trash. In Jesus's name, Amen.

Application

1. Be honest with yourself; what is a façade you have been trying to keep up?

2. What does that façade expose about you?

3. What is your perception of someone struggling with the things you keep hidden?

4. Release yourself from your ideology of perfection and say aloud, "God's grace is all I need. In my weakness, His strength is perfect" (2 Corinthians 12:9).

Make Notes Here:

Biblical Roots for Your Week

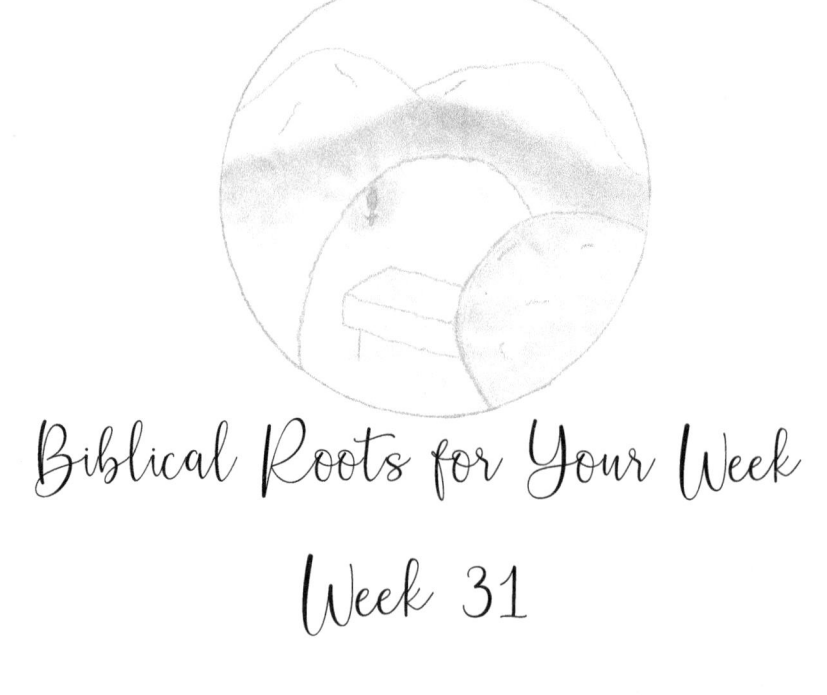

Week 31

God activates my rescue mission when I speak the opposite of my dire circumstances.

Magnetic Words

"Magnets" have a *north* and a south pole. These opposite poles "attract" each other. However, the same poles go against each other; in other words, they "repel" each other. Your words concerning your circumstances operate just like a "magnet." We, as Christians, are called to speak about those things that have not come to pass as though they already have.[102] How is this like a magnet? Well, when you speak the opposite of your situation, you are "attracting" to your life

---

[102] Romans 4:17 (KJV)

the thing in which you spoke. The *north* pole (God) connects with the south pole (your faith) and the "attraction" becomes "magnetic." This is especially true when you speak the Word of God over your situation—His word doesn't return unto Him void, but it accomplishes that which pleases Him and prospers you for whom He sent it.[103]

Well, how is this analogous to when a magnet repels? When the same poles connect, they "repel." Therefore, if you speak negativity or give life to your terrible circumstances—throwing a pity party and ruminating on that thing which seems to be keeping you down—then you stay down. This "repels" your spiritual growth, purpose, and, ultimately, hinders your desired successes. The Word of God discourages us from this because God, in His infinite wisdom, knows that "death and life are in the power of the tongue."[104] That scripture relayed in the message version warns that our words are either poison or fruit, but we get to choose.

I encourage you today to choose life. Speak not what you see, but what you hope. Mix that with faith and see God's "magnetic" attraction. You shall have what you say![105] Let's be sure to magnetize our words!

LaKeesha Griffin, God's pupil

Prayer

Lord, the Author and Finisher of my faith, I, (put your name here), thank you that you know my beginning and my end, and I thank you that you are orchestrating all those things

---

[103] Isaiah 55:11
[104] Proverbs 18:21 (KJV)
[105] Mark 11:22–24

in between. Lord, you have a perfect plan for how I should operate in my faith. Your plan is that my faith is directly connected to my words. I acknowledge that my words have a direct impact on what you perform in my life. I repent that I have not spoken the things I hope; instead, I have often spoken of defeat. I repent that because of the words I speak, I am delaying the manifestation of victory in my life. Lord, I want my words to magnetize to your power. I ask you, Father, to guard my mouth. I ask, Father, that you give me a new heart so that the words that come out of my mouth are those of hope and confidence that you are working it all out. Thank you for the victory in advance. Now Lord, here I am, willing and able to do your will and speak those things that you are manifesting in the spiritual realm so I may reap the joy of it in the natural realm. In Jesus's name, Amen.

Application

1. What are some negative things you say about yourself or someone else close to you (i.e., a spouse or child, a situation, a task, a dream, etc.)?

2. For every negative thing you list, write down something positive you can say that reflects your desired hope for that thing.

3. Be intentional to find a scripture that will keep you hopeful about it working out for your own good.

4. Every time you think something negative about that thing, say the scripture instead.

5. Keep a log of how each thing changed once you changed your words about it.

Make Notes Here:

Biblical Roots for Your Week

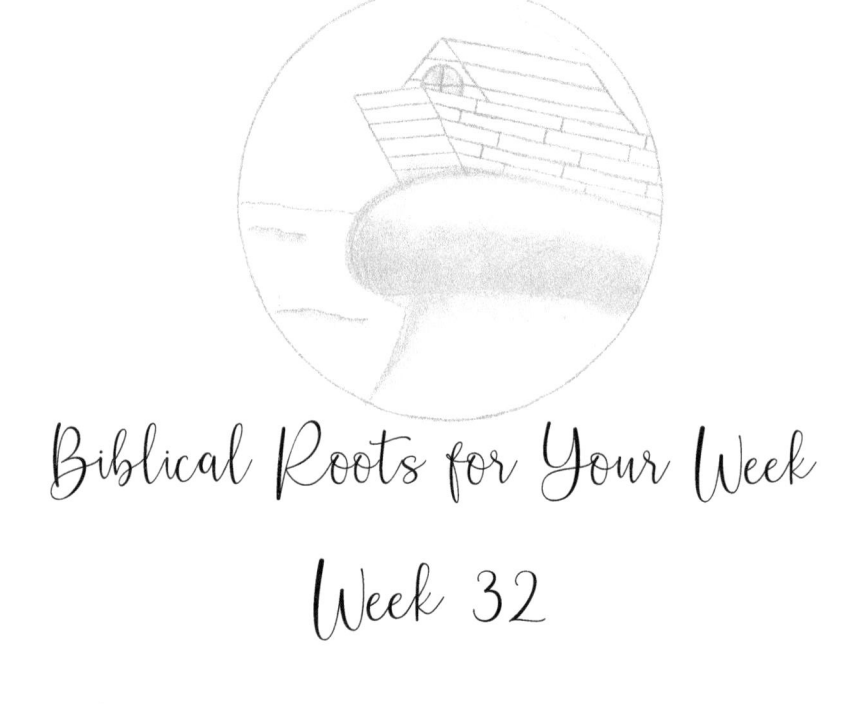

Week 32

My life is a compilation of times I allowed Jesus to mold me from nothing into something.

A Gift for God

It amazes me how my youngest son is so eager to present what he has worked on throughout the day to his dad at the end of the day. He takes a stack of Legos that he turns into a spaceship, some schoolwork he had difficulty grasping but later has mastered, or a picture he drew from "nothing" and presents it with great "joy" just to hear his dad say, "Well done." Jesus does the same with His Father, God.

The Word of God informs us that Jesus is able to keep us from falling and to present us faultless before the Father with "exceeding joy."[106] Jesus, too, thrives off of pleasing His Father. He takes what the world deems as "nothing" and changes us into "something" to behold before the Father. He does this with "exceeding joy" because He knows all the ins and outs for us to become *faultless* before God. And it is only by His doing because He is the only one able to prevent us from falling so that He can present us faultless.

You see, Jesus is working on your heart, your mind, and your very soul right now. He is working on you, the "nothing" thrown away by your family because you went wayward in sin. He is working on you, the "nothing" who seems to think your life has no purpose. He is working on you, the "nothing" who hasn't outwardly received Him as your Lord and Savior. He is working 24/7 so the "nothing" that the world disregarded can be presented before His Father. He will do this with "exceeding joy" because it gives Him pleasure that you, the "nothing" (by the world's terms), may be counted among those worthy of the Kingdom of God.[107]

When Jesus is in it, we are never a "nothing," because it is *not a thing* for Him to be exceedingly above all we ask or think.[108] He'll say, "Dad, look how I turned what the world thought was 'nothing' into 'something.'" Rest assured, He is working on you, in you, and through you.

LaKeesha Griffin, God's Pupil

---

[106] Jude 1:24-25 (KJV)
[107] 2 Thessalonians 1:5
[108] Ephesians 3:20

Prayer

Lord, the Son of God, I, (put your name here), thank you that you delight in pleasing your Father. I thank you that you have taken the charge wholeheartedly to mold me so that I may be presented faultless before your Father and my God. Thank you for working on my heart, mind, and soul. I know you are working so that I am a reflection of you. Lord, I repent for giving into the world's idea that I am nothing. Despite what the world thinks I lack, I am something because I am in Jesus Christ. Lord, I repent that I have not been intentional to do what is pleasing to you like you do what is pleasing for your Father in Heaven. Now Lord, I ask you to deposit within my heart the knowledge that I am something because you have called me and given me purpose. I ask that you help me believe that you have plans for me, plans to prosper me, not to harm me, and to give me hope for today and a future for tomorrow. Now Lord, here I am, willing and able to do your will and be like you in doing what is pleasing unto our Father. In Jesus's name, Amen.

Application

1. List all the things the world (parents, boss, co-workers, friends, etc.) has said to you that made you feel like you were nothing.

2. For everything you list, find a scripture that reveals what God thinks about you—that you are something.

3. Anytime those thoughts that you are nothing come up, recite aloud those scriptures.

4. Continue to pray that you see yourself as God sees you.

Make Notes Here:

Biblical Roots for Your Week

Week 33

As I draw closer to Jesus, I am reminded I am drawing closer to the Heart of God.

The Heart of the Father

Have you seen pictures of God depicted this way?: God is a gigantic being sitting on a supreme throne with what it looks like a microscopic person standing before His throne. This is far from the truth and only paints an unrealistic picture of our God. Moreover, this perpetuates misconceptions of God—that He is too big, so unreachable, and jumps to the judgment to condemn. The Word of God depicts it differently: God sits on a "throne of grace," where we find "mercy."[109]

---

[109] Hebrews 4:16

So how could a "throne of grace" where God readily hands out "mercy" to his children be depicted so terrifyingly? Well, I hate to say it, but I hear the elders in the church yelling, "Tell the truth! Shame the devil!" The truth is this: those who depict God as such and think of God as an almighty being who is too big, so unreachable, and jumps to judgment to condemn, do not really know the "Heart of the Father"; and as such, they do not have a relationship with Him at all.

The "Heart of the Father" is to give us grace and mercy in our time of need.[110] The "Heart of the Father" is to be close to the brokenhearted and those crushed in spirit.[111] The "Heart of the Father" is for us, not against us.[112] Why? Well, that's simple. The Word of God enlightens us: the "Heart of the Father" is Jesus.

Jesus exists at the very "Heart of the Father."[113] Hebrews 4:16 instructs us to approach God's "throne of grace" with confidence. We can do this because we have Jesus, who empathizes with our weaknesses.[114] We can be confident before the throne of God because we carry to the throne Jesus, the "Heart of the Father."

Those who do not carry Jesus, the "Heart of the Father," with them to the "throne of grace" will steadily see God as a gigantic being sitting on a supreme throne and remain feeling like a microscopic person. Why? Because what you don't know always seems too big. Get to know Jesus, the "Heart of the Father," so you can go confidently before the "throne of grace," where you will find "mercy."

LaKeesha Griffin, God's pupil

---

[110] Hebrews 4:16
[111] Psalm 34:18 (NIV)
[112] Romans 8:31
[113] John 1:18 (MSG)
[114] Hebrews 4:14–16

Prayer

Lord, the King of Glory, I, (put your name here), thank you that you sit on an approachable throne of grace. I thank you that if I come to your throne with confidence, I can find grace and mercy there. I thank you that you gave me your very heart, Jesus, so that I can approach your throne and receive grace and mercy in my time of need. Thank you for drawing near to me when I am brokenhearted and crushed in spirit. And thank you for being for me, not against me. Lord, I repent that I have too often perceived you as a God who is too big, unapproachable, unreachable, and eager to condemn me. Lord, I repent that I have not truly seen the Heart of the Father, Jesus. Lord, I ask you to reveal more of your heart to me through your scripture. Help me to see that you love me so much that you rejoice over me with joy and singing. Now Lord, here I am, willing and able to do your will and approach your throne of grace with confidence. In Jesus's name, Amen.

Application

1. Be honest with yourself; how do you perceive God?

2. Be honest with yourself; how do you perceive Jesus?

3. Write down anything you have not been confident to bring to God's throne of grace.

4. Be intentional to study more about the Heart of the Father, Jesus. Then, revisit your perception about God, the Father, and Jesus, the Son.

Make Notes Here:

Biblical Roots for Your Week

Week 34

God's interrogations are purposed to question my soul, grow my faith, and lead me on a righteous path.

God Answers

A leading question guides or prompts the person being asked to a specific answer. In short, the answer is within the question because the question is suggestive. It is a very cunning way to conduct dialogue, because a leading question gives the person being asked no room for an alternative response. It hinders all open-ended responses.

God asks us leading questions all the time. Don't believe me? Well, God said: don't you know that you're the temple of the Holy Spirit, and I (your God) dwell in your midst?[115] Haven't I commanded you to be strong and courageous, not afraid or discouraged, for I (your God) am with you always?[116] Don't you want to get well?[117] What, could you not watch and pray with me for just one hour?[118] "You of little faith, why are you so afraid?"[119]

God asks suggestively because He is not looking for your excuses. He doesn't want you to ruminate on being abandoned, neglected, and abused. He doesn't want to hear your excuse that no one is helping you get in the pool to receive your long-awaited healing.[120] Why? Because He said that though your mother and father forsake you, He has received and accepted you.[121] He doesn't want you to dwell on your prior or future circumstances at all. He asks you leading questions for you to affirm who you are in His Kingdom—to get you to realize that you can call on the same power that resurrected Jesus from the grave.

With the leading questions, God is giving you the answer that He lives in your temple.[122] He is giving you the answer to walk in strength and courageousness.[123] He is giving you the answer that you can be healed if you just believe.[124] He is giving you the answer that you must remain vigilant

---

[115] 1 Corinthians 3:16 (NIV)
[116] Joshua 1:9
[117] John 5:6
[118] Matthew 26:40–41 (KJV)
[119] Matthew 8:26 (NIV)
[120] John 5:7
[121] Psalm 27:10
[122] 1 Corinthians 3:16
[123] Joshua 1:9
[124] John 5:6

in prayer and watch for your breakthrough.[125] He is giving you the answer to always operate in enough faith to be free from fear.[126]

God's leading questions operate to affirm us and reaffirm our faith. In this sense, the question marks in God's leading questions should be seen more as periods, because they are operating as a statement or command. God is just leading you to remember whose you are; there are no alternative responses or excuses that can combat that. God's leading questions are leading you! Just find your God and His power in the inquiry!

LaKeesha Griffin, God's pupil

Prayer

Lord, the Captain of my ship, I, (put your name here), thank you that you are leading me through the storms of life. I thank you that through your words, you help me to affirm my position in your Kingdom and to reaffirm my own faith. You are magnificent. Lord, I repent that I have made a lot of excuses that, in hindsight, have hindered my progression in my faith and victory in my circumstances. I repent that I have concentrated too much on the tree in my way instead of believing, by faith, that I can speak to the tree, and it will wither away. I repent that I often cower in the trial instead of being intentional to speak my faith to the trial. Lord, help me to see you as bigger than the trial. Help me to see how you are leading me through the trial by immersing myself in your word and opening my eyes and ears to your great counsel.

---

[125] Matthew 26:40
[126] Matthew 8:26

Now Lord, here I am, willing and able to do your will and allow your inquisition to lead me. In Jesus's name, Amen.

Application

1. What are some things you believe to be an obstacle (or are in your way) in your life (i.e., sickness and disease, lack of education, depleted finances, relationship woes, etc.)?

2. For every obstacle you list, find a scripture that reminds you of the promises of God pertaining to overcoming the obstacle and receiving the victory.

3. Now, write a leading question for yourself using the scripture you found for each respective obstacle. The leading question should remind you of the promises of God in that scripture. For example, if you are living in shame from a past sin and feel disconnected from God, you could write the following: does the Lord not say that nothing can separate me from His love?

4. Continue to pray, being intentional in your prayers to remind yourself of the promises of God.

Make Notes Here:

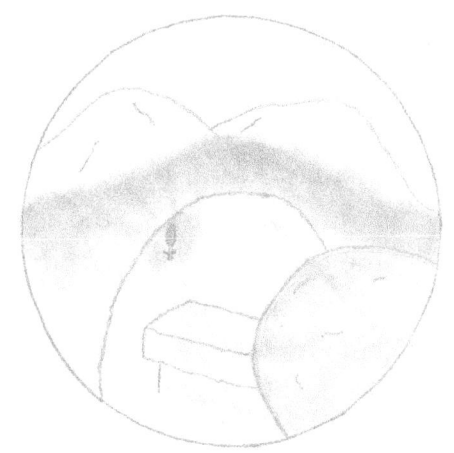

Biblical Roots for Your Week

Week 35

The will of the Father is that I am persistent before His throne, even if it is to persuade Him to choose a different path for me.

Persistence is Persuasive

My son tends to be persistent when he wants something. He advocates for himself in how he has been obedient, made good grades, or even helped someone else. Some may consider this to be self-seeking for the benefit of getting what he wants, but I know it resembles how we are supposed to be persistent before our Father—never giving up, without fail. Why? Because persistence is faith.

Read the next sentence slowly so that it will get in your soul: *you have the ability to change the will of the Father.* Think about it this way: "But for your faith!" You see, your faith is the sweet-smelling fragrance unto God's nostrils.[127] Like something good cooking in the kitchen, the aroma itself may cause one to reconsider another portion. God, too, desires your faith to be the sweet-smelling fragrance unto His nostrils because it causes Him to reconsider His will for your life. Don't believe me? Let's look at the evidence.

God told Abraham to sacrifice his only son. But Abraham's son, Isaac, was spared.[128] Why? "But for Abraham's faith!" God had decided to do away with humanity because of humanity's disobedience and tarnished hearts.[129] But humanity was spared. Why? "But for Noah's faith!" God wanted to punish the Israelites for their disobedience. But the Israelites were spared.[130] Why? "But for Moses's faith!" God told King Hezekiah to put his house in order because he was about to die. But King Hezekiah was spared and lived 15 more years.[131] Why? "But for King Hezekiah's faith!" You see, King Hezekiah prayed to God, saying, "Remember, Lord, how I have walked before you faithfully and with wholehearted devotion and have done what is good in your eyes."[132] King Hezekiah remained persistent, reminding God of his faithfulness and obedience.

Just as God changed His will for these chosen people, He can do the same for you. He can extend your life, like

---

[127] 2 Corinthians 2:15 (AMP)
[128] Genesis 22:12
[129] Genesis 6:9–22
[130] Exodus 32:11–14
[131] 2 Kings 20:4–6
[132] 2 Kings 20:3 (NIV)

He did for King Hezekiah, extend provision, like He did for Abraham, and extend forgiveness, like He did for all humanity and the Israelites because of Noah and Moses. I encourage you to stay persistent and remind God of your faith in Him! "X" may be His will "but for your faith!"

LaKeesha Griffin, God's pupil

Prayer

Lord, the Alpha and Omega, I, (put your name here), thank you that you have my life and future in your hands. I thank you that you consider my persistence in coming to you as true faith. I thank you that you look upon me with grace and mercy when I come to you; then, you choose, according to my faith, to amend your will. I acknowledge that your will is perfect for my life. Lord, I repent that I have not had a *but for my faith* approach to my trials and tribulations. I repent that instead of being persistent and allowing my faith to be a sweet-smelling fragrance unto you nostrils, I often give up before the breakthrough. Lord, I ask you to help me be persistent in my prayers. I ask you to remind me that my faith is my passport to approach your throne of grace with confidence. Now Lord, here I am, willing and able to do your will and be persistent before your throne. In Jesus's name, Amen.

Application

1. Think about what you do exceptionally well. Then, list your gifts and talents.
2. Draft what you think God's will is for your life based on your list of gifts and talents.

3. Go to prayer with your list, and ask God to reveal whether you are correct about His will for your life.

4. Be persistent in praying to God that He reveals those things which are hidden; don't give up until you get your answers.

5. Amend your list once His will is revealed to you. Also, be willing to plead to God to amend His will for your life.

Make Notes Here:

Biblical Roots for Your Week

Week 36

I refuse to accept a knockout when there's a reprieve awaiting me.

The Fight for My Life

A "knockout" is something serious in the sport of boxing. Fans watch and estimate in which round the more inexperienced and oftentimes younger boxer will be "knocked out." A "knockout" is when one boxer administers such a blow to the opposing boxer that he/she can't get up again to effectively resume the match, and thus, by default, the match is terminated and the one who administers the "knockout" is declared victorious. Alternatively, when a boxer gives up (surrenders) or the referee determines that boxer's inability to continue the fight, it is called a "technical knockout." I ask you: what would it take for you to give up your fight against your opposer?

The Word of God commands us to never give up. "Let us not become weary in doing good, for at the proper time we will reap a harvest if we do not give up."[133] I emphasize this scripture purposefully. It seems intuitive to give up on the one thing that causes us weariness, mental and physical harm, and stress. When running a marathon, one might want to give up when they feel their exhaustion set in—the heat from miles of running, the pain in their legs from the continual steps striking along the pavement, and the mental fight that it's just not worth it in the end. But do you know that the one running the marathon has another choice? When the marathon runner feels the weariness setting in, he/she can simply choose to walk. Just like the boxer can use his opponent's shoulder or the boxing ring's ropes to rest, we must find avenues for a reprieve so that we don't give up.

I say this with all earnestness as I fight with my body suffering from a disease that affects my body's major organs. Declare it with me for yourself: the enemy will not get an opportunity to parade around the boxing ring with a boxing belt proclaiming a "knockout" over me. Nor will I surrender or have an outsider tell me I can't fight anymore, calling for a "technical knockout."

In a season of weariness—suffering mental and physical stress, sickness/disease, and so on—we must rest on God's promises. We must find a word that bolsters our confidence that we will get the victory and that the opposer, our enemy, will get "knocked out." My verse is this: "my flesh and my heart may fail, but God is the strength of my heart and my

---

[133] Galatians 6:9 (NIV)

portion forever."[134] What about you? What will you do when you get weary? Give up and accept a "knockout"? Or continue to fight and stand on God's word?

LaKeesha Griffin, God's pupil

Prayer

Lord, my Refuge, Help, and Strength, I, (put your name here), thank you that I rest in your arms, and there I find safety from the combativeness of life. I thank you that when I am in a fight, you give me a reprieve so I may continue the fight. I know the race is not given to the swift, nor the battle to the strong, but to the one who endures until the end. Lord, I thank you that you have promised to finish what you started in me until the end. Now Lord, I repent that oftentimes, I have tapped out of the ring for fear that I will be knocked out. I repent that at other times, I fail to put up a resistance against the enemy, and, by doing that, I am technically being knocked out. I ask you, Lord, to help me fight. Please, Father, help me to be victorious against the wiles of the enemy who is trying to keep me from receiving the glory in knocking Him out. Now Lord, here I am, willing and able to do your will and put up a fight. In Jesus's name, Amen.

Application

1. What fight(s) have you tapped out of (surrendered) in the fighting ring of life?

2. If you had continued to fight, what do you think would have been the end result(s)?

---

[134] Psalms 73:26 (NIV)

3. What current fights are you facing?

4. Write down the following: "I will not accept a knockout in (insert the current fights you are facing)!" Now, say it aloud.

5. When you feel like you can't fight anymore, revisit what you wrote down and be intentional to continue to say aloud your impending victory.

Make Notes Here:

Biblical Roots for Your Week

Week 37

The inheritance that I have yet to see has value beyond man's definition of abundance.

The Abundant Life

Did you know you are richly blessed? No, really, you truly are! The Word of God says we are heirs, and as heirs, we have an inheritance. God promises that His children obtain an "inheritance that can never perish, spoil, or fade."[135] Well, you say you are struggling here on Earth and don't feel richly blessed; and if you have such an inheritance, how can you obtain the bank account access to that inheritance? Our inheritance is not kept here on Earth. Our inheritance

---

[135] 1 Peter 1: 4 (NIV)

is kept in Heaven for us.[136] We have an eternal or "heavenly inheritance." Just think—if it were kept here on Earth, it would be subjected to perishing, spoiling, fading, and maybe even being stolen from us. God wants our inheritance to be secured by Him because the inheritance that awaits us came at a cost.

A Last Will and Testament gives the one making the Will the authority to bequeath what is left upon their death to the one they deem worthy of that inheritance. Jesus perfected His Last Will and Testament when He died on the Cross for us. And it is by His death on the Cross and our belief in Him that we receive our eternal or "heavenly inheritance." Again, I tell you, you are richly blessed!!! But let me let you in on some eternal soul-saving advice.

Jesus's Will comes with some contingencies, like most other Wills. The contingency is this: we must deny ourselves, take up our own cross, and follow Jesus[137] by nailing our fleshly passions and desires to our cross.[138] In other words, Jesus's death bequeaths an eternal or "heavenly inheritance" only to those willing to crucify their flesh.[139]

If we are truly His children, then we are "heirs—heirs of God and joint heirs with Christ, [and] indeed we suffer with Him, that we may also be glorified together."[140] This gives a new meaning to the phrase, "I am rich in Jesus!"

LaKeesha Griffin, God's pupil

---

[136] 1 Peter 1:4
[137] Matthew 16:24
[138] Galatians 5:24
[139] Galatians 5:24
[140] Romans 8:17 (NKJV)

Prayer

Lord, my Sanctifier, Jehovah Mekaddishken, I, (put your name here), thank you that you have set me apart and consecrated me to receive an eternal inheritance. I thank you that when you died on the cross for my sins, you wrote my name in your will as an heir jointly with Christ. And Lord, I thank you that you are keeping my inheritance safely in Heaven so it is not subjected to spoiling, perishing, or fading away. I acknowledge that because you are safely keeping it, my receipt of the inheritance is inevitable. Lord, I repent that I have looked for how the world can richly bless me, taking on the world's status of who I am because of what I have in my natural bank account. I repent that I have taken for granted that there is no worldly value to the bank account you have given me. I will no longer take what you have bequeathed to me for granted. I will take up my cross, deny myself, and follow you so that I may receive the glory with you in Heaven. Now Lord, here I am, willing and able to do your will and receive my heavenly inheritance. In Jesus's name, Amen.

Application

1. What are some things you indulge in of the world that you need to deny yourself?

2. Have you received Jesus (in your heart) as your Lord and Savior? If not, why?

3. Make a choice today to take up your cross, deny yourself, and follow Jesus.

4. Write this, then say it aloud (preferably with someone else so they can be your prayer and

accountability partner): Lord, I have sinned. Please forgive me. I believe in my heart you died on the Cross for my sins. I believe you rose from the dead. I wish to walk a righteous path, take up my cross, deny myself, and follow you. I invite you into my heart and to take control of my life. I put all of my trust in you as my Lord and Savior. In Jesus's name, Amen.

Make Notes Here:

Biblical Roots for Your Week

Week 38

When I sort through the lines of my connections, I realize why I suffer from power drainage.

Disconnect Notice

The word "power" has multiple meanings. It could refer to someone with authority to act in a particular way, someone with physical strength, or a "source of energy." Let's take the latter definition because it is most essential to our Christian journey. Our "power" is affected by our "source of energy." During the summer months, we are faced with high power bills because we run the air conditioner nonstop to fight the extreme summer heat. Unbeknownst to most, the power company provides tips all the time on how to conserve our "power" or our "source of energy." For example, Alabama

Power suggests that to be cost-effective, we should unplug appliances that are not in use. Well, why is it cost-effective to unplug an idle appliance? One would assume that an idle appliance does not require power. One may assume that an appliance only requires power when we press the "on" switch. Well, this is not the case.

The truth of the matter is this: though physically idle, if something is still connected to the source (you), it is using (your) power. Accordingly, the logical conclusion would be that if you want to save on power, you must completely disconnect from what you are attached to in order to avoid power drainage. Now, I ask you, who or what are you connected to? Better said, who or what are you allowing to be connected to you?

The Word of God instructs us to keep away from any brother who is walking in idleness and not in accord with what we have learned via our Lord Jesus Christ.[141] It says we should have nothing to do with those who appear godly but deny God's power.[142] Why should we stay away? Why do we need to avoid what is idle? Because what is idle can still take our power. "Bad company corrupts good morals."[143] If we walk with the wise, we become wise; if we walk in the companion of fools, we will suffer harm.[144] It stands, then, that we should terminate our connections that give us a high power bill. I encourage you today to send them their disconnect notice! And make it effective immediately!

LaKeesha Griffin, God's pupil

---

[141] 2 Thessalonians 3:6 (NIV)
[142] 2 Timothy 3:5
[143] 1 Corinthians 15:33 (AMP)
[144] Proverbs 13:20 (NIV)

Prayer

Lord, my Power Source, I, (put your name here), thank you that you are omnipotent yet gracious enough to allow me to be connected to you. I realize you are connected to me by my faith. So, I thank you that as long as I am connected to you through my faith, I have power to speak to the mountain, and then you will move the mountain out of my way. Lord, I repent that I have been connected to others who have drained my power. They have not contributed anything to my stable connection with you. Instead, they have attempted to lure me away and become disconnected from you. I ask you to give me the courage to terminate those connections that drain my power. I ask you to remove those people in my life who are idle but relying on my power. After I send them their disconnect notice, help them to then connect to you. Now Lord, here I am, willing and able to do your will and disconnect from those idle in my life. In Jesus's name, Amen.

Application

1. Write the names of those who you think are idle in your life (draining your power and never reciprocating healthy contributions).

2. Think back to the onset of the relationship. Has it always been a one-sided, idle relationship (that is, have they ever contributed anything to your faith walk)?

3. Do you believe that because they rely on you so much, you have not given them an opportunity to walk on their own in a path to finding a true relationship with Christ?

4. If the answers to the above are "yes," consider terminating your relationship with these people with the hope that they find Jesus and establish a true connection with Him.

Make Notes Here:

Biblical Roots for Your Week

Week 39

Despite much effort, the trash I conceal on the inside finds its way out.

The Trash Container

We put trash in trash cans and routinely take it out to the bigger trash can to be collected by the sanitation department. If we leave trash in the trash can for too long, though the trash can has a lid, the collection of smells from all that was leftover and not of good use anymore begins to find its way outward. In other words, *though neatly kept and packaged, trash on the inside always manifests on the outside.* Read that last sentence again! In fact, we routinely take trash out to be collected because if not for the frequency of trash collection, the smell would be overbearing and even unhealthy. Likewise, if we keep the trash from our lives (heartbreak, past sins and mistakes, neglect from others, abandonment, etc.) on the inside, it eventually manifests on the outside. It is imperative that just like taking our physical trash out to be collected by the sanitation department, we should take our souls' trash to the ultimate trash collector and destroyer of all things unfruitful. If we fail to do this, the issues of life will be revealed, "for the mouth speaks what the heart is full of."[145]

God encourages us to bring our trash to Him: "Come to me all you who are weary and burdened, and I will give you rest."[146] Once we come to Him, we then give Him our trash by confessing our sins, for "if we confess our sins, He is faithful and just and will forgive us our sins and purify us from ALL unrighteousness."[147] Sometimes, we may have stored our trash too long, and the only way to get the smell out is to deeply cleanse it—like when you put some Clorox and/or soap in the trash can and just let it sit outside for an extended time. When we sit in our trash for too long, it saturates our souls; we then need to be deeply cleansed. The only one who can do that is God, for He promised that "though your sins are like scarlet, they shall be as white as snow; though they are red as crimson, they shall be like wool."[148] Only God can turn the tainted and corruptible into the untainted and incorruptible.

I encourage you to give your weariness and burdens (trash) to Him. I encourage you to confess your sins to our Merciful Father. It is with frequently giving our soul's trash to Him that we see the manifestation of a pure (clean) heart

---

[145] Matthew 12:34; Luke 6:45
[146] Matthew 11:28 (NIV)
[147] 1 John 1:9 (NIV)
[148] Isaiah 1:18 (NIV)

and a steadfast spirit.[149] I ask you: does your soul's trash need to be emptied? Let God empty all of it and deeply cleanse your soul!

LaKeesha Griffin, God's pupil

Prayer

Lord, my Righteousness, Jehovah Tsidkenu, I, (put your name here), thank you that you collect and destroy my soul's trash if I just bring it to you. I thank you that, though I may be weary and burdened from all I endure in the world, I have can have a new start when I give it all to you. Thank you for exchanging my weariness and heavy burden so that I may receive your yoke, which is easy, and your burden, which is light. Lord, I repent that I have not allowed you to reset my soul as I should. I have often carried along, ruminating in the trash; I have allowed it to manifest on the outside, and it has affected my most important relationships, productivity, and faith. Please forgive me, Father. As I receive your forgiveness, I know my trash that was like scarlet is being made white as snow. Thank you for pressing my reset button. I ask you to remind me of when I need to bring my soul's trash to you. Now Lord, here I am, willing and able to do your will and pledge to give what is trash in my life to you, the ultimate trash collector. In Jesus's name, Amen.

Application

1. Make a list of the things (i.e., abandonment, neglect, abuse, being a victim of rape or molestation, etc.) you deal with inwardly that

---

[149] Psalm 51:10

manifest outwardly in your interactions with others.

2. List the relationships those things you listed are affecting.

3. Have you exposed those things to God, asking for healing from the thing that happened to you and the resulting insecurities and feelings it left?

4. Expose those things now. Confidently go before God's throne of grace and give it to Him; write this, then say it aloud: Lord, I, (insert your name here), have been suffering internally from (name all of those things you included in your list). It has manifested outwardly, causing confusion and chaos in my relationship with (name the relationships you listed). Lord, I repent for not bringing it to you. I ask that you heal not only my brokenness, but also heal and restore my relationship(s). I receive it all now. In Jesus's name, Amen.

Make Notes Here:

Biblical Roots for Your Week

Week 40

To be connected to the indestructible vine means I bear fruit in all seasons.

Impervious

Jesus is our true vine. If we remain as a branch in the true vine, we will bear much fruit.[150] We have a neighbor who "cut down" a tree to a stump, I assume for beautification purposes. Well, one would think that if you cut a tree down to a stump, that would be the end of that tree. The tree, instead, has miraculously and outwardly expressed, "I still have life in me!" This tree has caused branches to grow up from the ground. Just think about it, a "cut-down" tree with the ability

---

[150] John 15:1–5

to grant life to new branches. Yes, you guessed it. Jesus is the "cut-down" tree. He was "cut down" by His choice, yet He remains alive with all visibility ("Behold, my hands and feet. . .") of what He endured for our iniquities and sins.[151]

Like this tree, you, too, have been "cut down" by those who deem you unworthy, expendable, and maybe just in the way. You may have been "cut down" by mere words, actions, or inaction. You may have endured intolerance, a lack of gratitude for what you bring to a relationship or a job, or, were deemed unfit for something because, like Jesus, your scars from how you were mistreated are visible. However, their attempt to cut you down (and yes, I know it hurts) is just an attempt to get you disconnected from the true vine.

You see, you can be "cut down" and still declare, "I still have life in me!" However, that life can only bear fruit if you remain in Jesus, the true vine. Want to prove those who cut you down wrong? I am sure you do. Me, too. But you cannot do it without Jesus!

I ask you: what causes us to be in awe of a "cut-down" tree? The fact that after all it has endured, it still bears fruit because it remained connected to its life source, the vine. All you have to do is remain in the true vine; He is your source of a fruitful life! Remain in Him!

LaKeesha Griffin, God's pupil

Prayer

Lord, the True Vine, I, (put your name here), thank you that you are my life source. I thank you that as long as I am

---

[151] Luke 24:39–40

connected to you, it doesn't matter how many times I am cut down. Lord, I thank you that you show me it is okay to carry around visible reminders that I have been cut down. Like your wear your scars, I will not hide mine, because they are a reminder to the world of your grace and mercy that sustained me when the world thought I had no more life in me. I declare that there is still life in me because I remain connected to you. Lord, I repent that I have been ashamed of my own scars. I have often felt like damaged goods. But I know now that even damaged goods have a purpose; that is, they, too, have the same nourishing properties as any other fruit. I ask you to help me to proclaim all you have done for me by making my scars visible to the world. I ask you to make me an example of how you can revive all who are cut down. Now Lord, here I am, willing and able to do your will and reveal those things which once were broken in me that you healed. In Jesus's name, Amen.

Application

1. What visible or figurative scars do you carry around?

2. Do you try to hide them?

3. Write down the narrative of how you got each scar.

4. Seeking God's counsel, write down how He has healed those scar(s), causing you to bear fruit despite the scar(s).

5. Now, go show your scars to the world, telling others that though you were cut down, you were revived because you remained in the true vine.

Make Notes Here:

Biblical Roots for Your Week

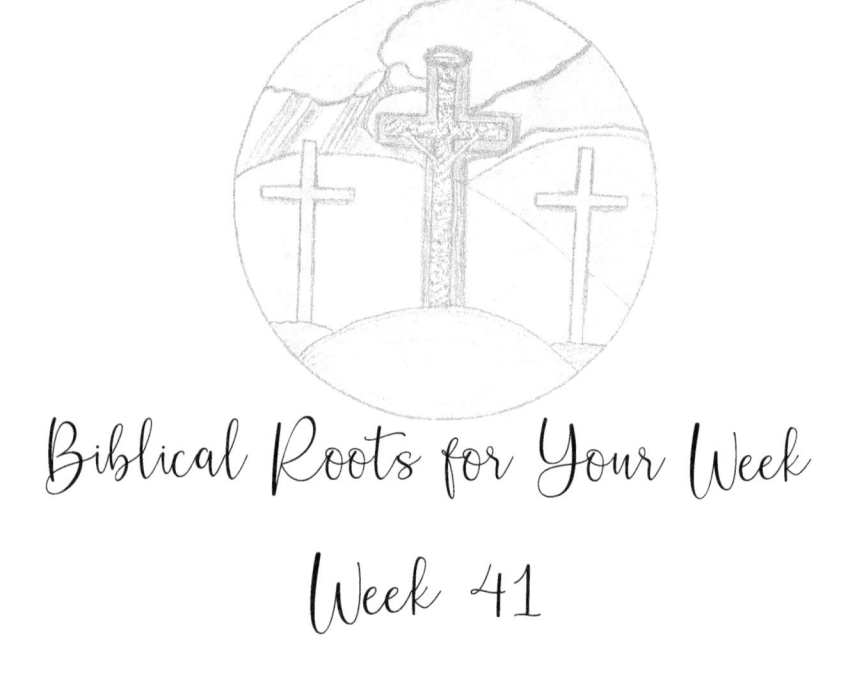

Week 41

Self-talk reflects an image I only see; it has the potential to stunt purpose or bolster courage, but I get to decide.

Belovedness

How you feel about yourself is a direct correlation to what you say to yourself, whether it is an inward or outward expression. "Words" are very critical to every aspect of our lives because "words" have the power to manifest here on Earth. Scripture reveals to us, "In the beginning was the Word, and the Word was with God, and the Word was God."[152] God thinks highly of "words." He uses "words" to build ("Through faith we understand that the worlds were

---

[152] John 1:1 (KJV)

framed by the word of God")[153] and to destroy that which is unfruitful (to the unfruitful fig tree Jesus said, "No man eat fruit of thee hereafter for ever," and the fig tree dried up from the roots).[154]

God responds to "words," especially His own. Don't believe me? He thought so highly of His "Word" that He manifested His "Word" here on Earth in Jesus: "And the Word was made flesh, and dwelt among us, (and we beheld His glory, the glory as of the only begotten of the Father) full of grace and truth."[155] This is why what we speak to God should be His "words," not our own.

What we speak to ourselves should be God's "words" also. For the Word of God manifested, and He said, "I am watching to see that my Word is fulfilled."[156] That means what you say, if it is God's "Word," will manifest in your life, just like Jesus, the Word, who manifested here on Earth. Yes, it takes great effort and introspection to identify the negative thoughts we speak to and over ourselves, but if we do and make a diligent effort to speak God's "word" over ourselves, then we are practicing "belovedness," or the self-love that God teaches us. You do believe He teaches self-love, right? Don't tell me you only believe He teaches self-sacrifice and the love of others. You are wrong! "Thou shalt love thy neighbor as THYSELF."[157] Accordingly, "loving thyself" is a part of the great and second commandment. Think on that!

I know, lately, you have been down and depressed, experiencing social and financial woes, feeling left out and maybe

---

[153] Hebrews 11:3 (KJV)
[154] Mark 11:12-21 (KJV)
[155] John 1:14 (KJV)
[156] Jeremiah 1:12 (NIV)
[157] Matthew 22:39 (KJV)

without purpose. Guess what? There's a word for that. I am encouraging you to practice "belovedness," which means if you put yourself directly in the "Word," God is faithful to perform what you speak. It goes like this: instead of just reading the scripture, use "I am," "I will," "me," or "I have." Feeling insecure or unsafe, say aloud: "I am confident that the good work God has begun in me will be completed."[158] Lacking purpose, say aloud: "I have been chosen and appointed to bear fruit."[159] Feeling guilty about your past sins, say aloud: "God has given me a new heart and put a new spirit in me."[160] Feeling disconnected, say aloud: "Nothing can separate me from His love."[161]

I ask you: are you speaking God's "word" to and over yourself?

LaKeesha Griffin, God's pupil

Prayer

Lord, my Maker, Jehovah Hoseenu, I, (put your name here), thank you that you had me fearfully and wonderfully made. I thank you that you know your creation well. There is nothing I can hide from you because you search the innermost parts of man. I thank you that you know my heart and show compassion towards me. I thank you that you draw nearer to me when I am brokenhearted and crushed in spirit. Even when I retreat from you, your love covers me. Lord, I repent that I fail to show compassion to myself. I have not been active in taking my thoughts captive and making them

---

[158] Philippians 1:6
[159] John 15:16
[160] Ezekiel 36:26
[161] Romans 8:38

obedient to your Word. I ask you to help me see myself as you made me. Help me see myself through your eyes, Father. Now Lord, here I am, willing and able to do your will and practice belovedness. In Jesus's name, Amen.

Application

1. List all the negative thoughts you have about yourself.

2. For every negative thought you listed, write a positive affirmation for each, practicing "belovedness" with the use of scripture. Use "I am," "I will," "me," or "I have."

3. Now say each affirmation you constructed aloud.

4. Designate a time throughout each day, preferably early morning, to practice belovedness and say your positive affirmations aloud.

Make Notes Here:

Biblical Roots for Your Week

Week 42

A renewed mind is when God uploads protection to kill the downloaded virus in the belief system.

The Belief System

Are you blessing or cursing? You have the power to bless or curse. Don't believe me? Well, you do. You see blessings and curses manifest using the same system—that is, our belief system. The process is as follows: 1) there is a word that goes forth (a seed); 2) it takes root in our heart; 3) if thought on over and over again (ruminating stimulates growth), it grows and becomes a manifestation of (a version of) truth about who we are or what we are to become; 4) it then becomes a full-fledged weed (or blossom); and 5) we begin to role play as if a script has been written for us in compliance with the blessing or curse. Curses are, therefore, where the belief system is corrupted; it's now a system with a downloaded virus. So, how do we uncorrupt or kill the virus in our belief system?

I heard a sermon once about a man who, as a child, was told that he wasn't going to amount to anything, so he began to role play and lived his life compliant to what was spoken over him—a life of defiance and total disregard for others. Then, when he was an adult, someone spoke the exact opposite to him, saying if he would just apply himself, he could really amount to something. Something within him immediately changed. What changed? His belief system. This man was living under a curse.

Jesus demonstrated how we are to speak against the impure spirit or the curse on our lives or on the lives of others: to the man possessed by a demon, an impure spirit, Jesus said, "Be quiet! Come out of him!"[162] The change was immediate. Jesus "drove out many demons," or those suffering from an impure spirit.[163] How did Jesus drive out the impure spirit? "Jesus rebuked the impure spirit."[164] He rebuked the impure spirit with words by attacking the foundation of the belief system; that is, the old roots were uprooted, and a new seed was planted. That same power is upon you.

The Word instructs you to "bless and do not curse."[165] Instead, God desires you to act like Him, uprooting the old and planting a new seed; you are to work toward killing the virus in your and others' belief systems. You are to rebuke the curse about who you (they) are and who you (they) are

---

[162] Mark 1:25 (NIV)
[163] Mark 1:32 (NIV)
[164] Luke 9:42 (NIV)
[165] Romans 12:14 (NKJV)

to become. Jesus gave you the "power and authority to drive out all demons."[166] All you have to do is speak the exact opposite of what seed was planted in you or in someone else.

I challenge you to get to the root of the belief system and make space for the blessings, not the curses. I also challenge you to be intentional to speak blessings and not curses over others. Don't misuse your power and authority!

LaKeesha Griffin, God's pupil

Prayer

Lord, the Gardener, I, (put your name here), thank you that you know everything that needs to take place in my life in order to uproot the negativity that I have allowed to be planted in my soul. I thank you that part of your plan is that I have been bestowed with power and authority to rebuke the impure spirit within me. I thank you that the power and authority you have given me extends to others, giving me social accountability to speak what your Word says to them. Lord, I repent that I have believed what someone else said about me instead of what your Word says about me. I repent that I have also been careless with my words, saying words of negativity to others that could be rooted in their souls, causing unhappiness with themselves and in their lives. Lord, I ask you to guard my heart and mind. Help me to think on that which is praiseworthy and of good report so that it emanates out of my mouth towards myself and others. Now Lord, here I am, willing and able to do your will and speak only blessings to myself and others. In Jesus's name, Amen.

---

[166] Luke 9:1 (NIV)

Application

1. What curses do you believe have been spoken over you?

2. What blessings do you believe have been spoken over you?

3. Conduct a self-assessment of your life; which one have you been more compliant with, the blessing(s) or the cursing(s)?

4. Write down names of those you believe you spoke curses over. Now, be intentional to say the exact opposite to them in a way that breaks the curse. For example, if you said, "You are not smart enough to accomplish that," to someone, instead say, "If you apply yourself and are disciplined in your goals, you will accomplish exactly what you set your heart on."

5. Continue to ask God for help, and choose to believe the blessings, not the curses, over your life.

Make Notes Here:

Biblical Roots for Your Week

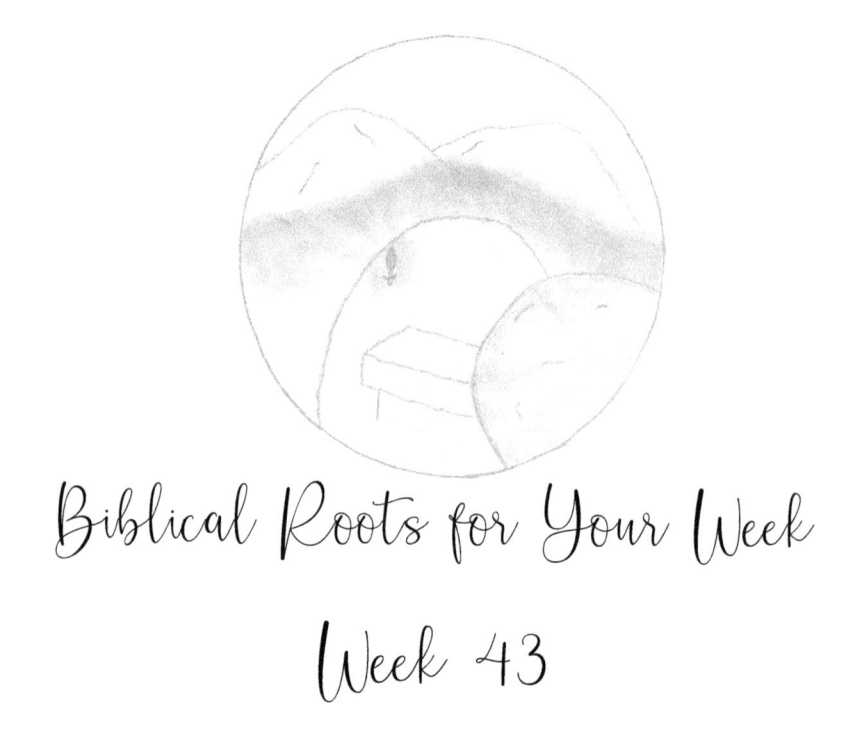

Week 43

Given an assignment I failed to complete, I still prevailed because God did the work.

An Assignment

Think back to when you were school-aged, and you were given a group assignment. The nature of group assignments is that every group member is required to participate and do an equal portion of the workload. However, that is rarely what happens. There is always that "one" who facilitates and, to prevent the assignment from not being turned in successfully to the teacher, will take it upon herself/himself to do the work under the pretense that all group members participate equally.

Jesus has been given an assignment, and His assignment is you! Jesus is that "one." Whether you are participating and working alongside Him—doing your required portion to bring the assignment to satisfactory completion so that it can be submitted before God—Jesus still works to see it to the end. "Because of your partnership in the gospel . . . being confident of this, that He who began a good work in you will carry it on to completion until the day of Christ Jesus."[167] Accordingly, He will facilitate you into your purpose, lead you around the mess and sin in your life, and bring it to satisfactory completion. And like the group members who get the good grade from the tireless efforts of the "one" who took it upon herself/himself to do the assignment alone, you get the glory. Why? Because Jesus has completed the assignment! Now you can say to God that the "good work" that was begun in you was finished.

So, you are not writing that book God told you to write a long time ago? Or you are running from being called to preach His Gospel? Maybe He told you to use your gift along with the pain from your past for a specific purpose (marriage ministry, prison ministry, or the outreach ministry for the homeless or women and children from abusive relationships). Whatever the good work He has begun in you (and yes, every single one of you has a good work that has been started in you), He is faithful to bring it to completion so you can get the good grade (glory) from His efforts.

LaKeesha Griffin, God's pupil

---

[167] Philippians 1:5-6 (NIV)

Prayer

Lord, my Master, Jehovah Adonai, I, (put your name here), thank you that you are the master of my future. I thank you that there is nothing you are unprepared for. Whatever you start, Father, you bring to completion. I thank you that you never sway in your assignment to keep me protected. Thank you for being the one who works on my behalf, even when I have thrown in the towel and wish to concede defeat. I know you will never let me give up because it is your desire to bring me before God without spot, blemish, or stain. Lord, I repent that I have taken our partnership for granted. I have allowed you to do all the work. It is you alone who are perfecting my faith. Help me to do the works required for my faith. Now Lord, here I am, willing and able to do your will and do my part in this partnership to receive glory. In Jesus's name, Amen.

Application

1. What assignment has God given you that you are stalled in bringing to completion?

2. Write a vision, including a timeline, for that assignment.

3. Tell someone close to you about the assignment and your vision for it. Ask that person to hold you accountable.

4. Schedule a frequency for evaluating that vision (i.e., weekly, bi-weekly, monthly, etc.). Make sure to amend your vision to reflect when you have met your goals.

5. Don't give up!

Make Notes Here:

Biblical Roots for Your Week

Week 44

Desperate for my needs to be fulfilled, I had no care for how loud my prayers appeared.

Loud Cries

Have you ever witnessed someone crying out in the spirit? If so, you may have seen them literally crying, screaming, dancing, or speaking in tongues. Others around them may seem baffled at what they are witnessing—maybe they've never witnessed it before, or they question the authenticity of the praise. When you are in desperate need or, more importantly, are in a posture of gratefulness and complete surrender, your environment doesn't matter. In other words, the "crowd" is a non-factor to your praise.

In Matthew 20:29–34, as Jesus was leaving Jericho, a large "crowd" followed him, and two blind men by the roadside shouted, "Lord Son of David, have mercy on us!" The "crowd" then rebuked the two blind men, which means the crowd outwardly expressed great disapproval and criticized them for their behavior and actions. The "crowd" then told them to be quiet.

Did the crowd's attempts to censure the two blind men change their behavior and actions? No; instead, the "crowd's" criticism of them caused them to "shout all the louder, 'Lord, Son of David, have mercy on us!'" So, what transpired afterwards? Jesus healed them completely. Matthew 20:34 says, "Jesus had compassion on them and touched their eyes. Immediately they received their sight and followed Him."

Whether you are in great need or greatly grateful, don't allow the "crowd" around you to dictate your cries out to God. If they rebuke you and/or tell you to be quiet, "shout all the louder!" Psalm 47:1 says, "Shout to God with cries of joy."

Shout!!! Jesus will respond with compassion and complete healing!

LaKeesha Griffin, God's pupil

Prayer

Lord, the One deserving of the Highest Praise, I, (put your name here), thank you that you hear my soft cries in the chaotic noise of the crowd around me. Lord, thank you for turning your ear to hear my cries and shining your face upon me. I am in desperate need of your healing touch right now. Lord, I cry out to you for complete healing. Where I am blind,

I ask you to cause me to see. Where I am unfruitful, I ask you to make fruitful. You have my complete surrender, Father. I am grateful for your healing touch, and I am confident that all areas of brokenness in my life are going to be completely healed. My trust is in you, Lord. Now, Lord help me to walk on a righteous path. Help me to not pay any attention to those naysayers around me. Help me to not consider the crowd around me as I continue to draw nearer to you and reach out for my blessings. Lord, I confess to you that I have paid too much attention to the crowd around me in my past. I have cared too much about what they thought of me and my relationship with you. I repent of this and ask for your forgiveness. Lord, consecrate me that I am set apart from those who do not care to know that you are the Almighty and loving God. I will shout to you, Lord, for my help comes from you only. Now, Lord, here I am, willing and able to do your will and shout despite the crowd around me. In Jesus's name, Amen.

Application

1. Compose a list of things you need healing from. (List #1)

2. Compose another list of reasons why you believe you have not received healing from those things in List #1. (List #2)

3. Bring both lists to prayer with you, asking God for the healing (List #1) and repenting for the reasons you have kept yourself from receiving complete healing (List #2).

4. Believe you will be healed.

5. Be bold and tell all those around you what you are believing in God for.

Make Notes Here:

Biblical Roots for Your Week

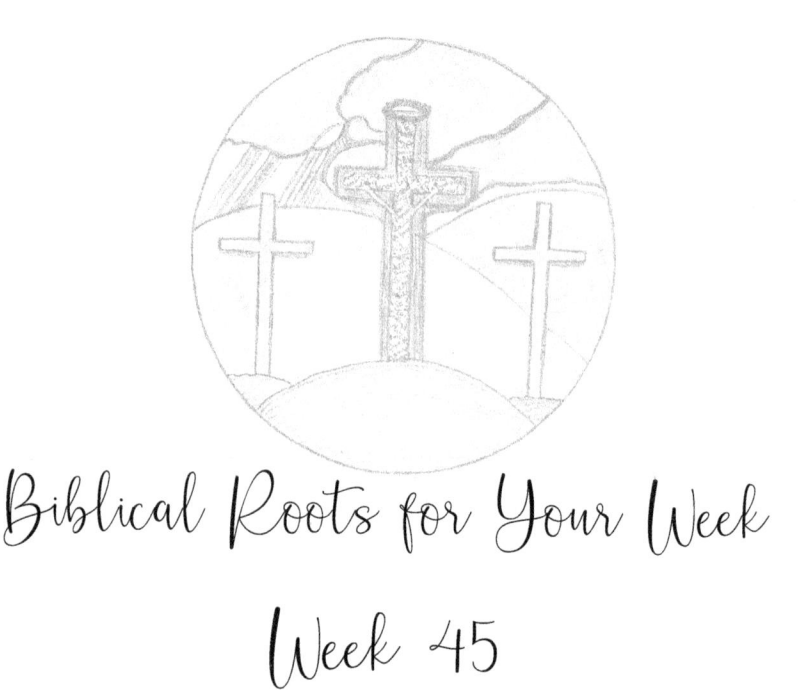

Week 45

No matter how massive the problem, the matter is never fixed.

Red Sea?

Problems? Well, we all have them. A problem is an unwelcome "matter" that poses some form of harm; however, in order to overcome it, it needs to be dealt with. Keep in mind, part of the definition for problem is "matter." "Matter" is literally everything around us. What's important to note is that "matter" can be manipulated or changed.

The children of Israel faced many problems; some problems were because of who they were as a people, and others were brought on by themselves. Despite the problems, God was their overall sufficiency. He made consistent provisions for them to sustain them "through" their problems. At the

Red Sea, as you can imagine, the children of Israel were in a state of despair. I can just about hear their moaning and groanings: how are we going to get over this problem? Why would God let us survive only to let us be destroyed by this? I ask you, have you made similar complaints? Well, I definitely have.

One thing so beautiful about what God did is that He changed the "matter"—The Red Sea—so that the children of Israel could walk not over, but "through" the Red Sea. Exodus 14:21–22 (KJV) informs, "And the Lord caused the sea to go back by a strong east wind all the night, and made the sea dry land, and the waters were divided. And the children of Israel went into the midst of the sea upon dry ground: and the waters were a wall unto them on their right hand, and on their left." I could imagine the children of Israel walking "through" the middle of it all on dry ground, hopefully being reminded that, as they walked past whales (big obstacles/problems) and shrimps (small obstacles/problems), what they deemed too hard of a problem could always be manipulated/changed by God for His glory. God is so awesome that He didn't even want them to walk through the Red Sea on a muddy path, but completely dry ground. It is my belief that He wanted to make sure there were no remnants of their old problems attached to them when they entered the promised land. He wanted their future to begin with a clean slate!

So, are you facing your Red Sea? Be reminded that God can change the whole "matter" you are facing. He will wall you completely off from your problems like He did for the children of Israel with the Red Sea. He will help you to walk "through" it so your future will begin with a clean slate.

Red Sea? No "matter." Truly nothing is impossible for God!

LaKeesha Griffin, God's pupil

Prayer

Lord, my Sufficiency, El Shaddai, I, (put your name here), thank you that despite the problems I face, you are faithful to provide for all of my needs. I thank you that everything I need is in you. Lord, I thank you that you are powerful to change the matter I am facing in such a way that the problem ceases to exist. And your goodness extends beyond the problem; you then make sure that there are no remnants in my life of my old problems. You give me a clean slate. Thank you, Father. Lord, I repent that I complain about the Red Seas in my life, magnifying the problems instead of magnifying your power to change the Red Seas completely. Please forgive me for not having enough faith in you to believe that if you brought me to the Red Sea, you'll get me through the Red Sea on dry ground. Lord, I ask you to keep my mind stayed on you and your power. Help me to look up to you, where my help comes from. Now Lord, here I am, willing and able to do your will and trust you to change the matter that I am facing. In Jesus's name, Amen.

Application

1. What are the problems—Red Seas—in your life?

2. Do you see a way to get through the Red Sea to the other side in your own human ability?

3. Have you partnered with God, giving the Red Sea entirely to Him?

4. If you haven't given it to God, do it now. If you have partnered with God, answer this

question honestly: have you complained about the problem(s) since you gave it to God?

5. Be faithful that God will change the matter you are facing by placing your complete trust in Him and refusing to complain. If you find yourself complaining, repent and give the problem(s) back to God.

Make Notes Here:

Biblical Roots for Your Week

Week 46

Fighting doesn't always connote physical action; it can also mean being completely still.

Fighting Fair?

We have a Great Dane, and as Great Danes are, she is huge. I never notice how much bigger she has gotten until we go for a walk and she is met with many dogs of different sizes and breeds. Our dog, Faith, will come close to another dog who is aggressively barking at her, and how does she respond? She doesn't bark, not once. Complete silence. It baffles me that my big dog doesn't feel the need to dominate by flaunting her size. Instead, she knows how to fight fair. She knows that her "stature" is enough. I tell you that your "stature" is enough.

Yes, stature can mean one's height. But I am not talking about that stature. Instead, I am talking about "stature," your reputation gained through your achievement via Christ. The question is then this: do you fight fair?

Jesus, when met with aggression, doubters, and even the impending Cross always, without fail, fought fair. He either quoted scripture or said nothing. In dialogue with the devil, Jesus continued to respond with "it is written," followed by the scripture itself: "man shall not live on bread alone, but on every word that comes from the mouth of God"[168]; "Do not put the Lord your God to the test"[169]; "Worship the Lord your God, and serve Him only."[170] Jesus stood silent amongst his accusers when He stood trial before Pilate. Pilate asked Jesus where He was from, and Jesus remained quiet. Pilate asked, "Do you refuse to speak to me? Don't you realize I have power either to free you or to crucify you?"[171] And yet while on the cross, Jesus said, "My God, my God, why have you forsaken me?"[172] This is a direct quote from scripture, Psalm 22:1.

I acknowledge that this is the right way to fight after failing miserably to do the same. When amounted with contention and aggression, I should have done like Jesus. What does responding like Jesus—a what would Jesus do/say strategy— yield? Well, for one, being quiet quiets the storm—"Peace, be still."[173] Why? Because, people rarely argue/contend with themselves. Alternatively, if you choose

---

[168] Matt 4:4 (NIV)

[169] Matt 4:7 (NIV)

[170] Matt 4:10 (NIV)

[171] John 19: 9–10 (NIV)

[172] Matthew 27:46 (NIV)

[173] Mark 4:39 (KJV)

to respond by quoting scripture, it ensures that you are responding to the situation with a biblical scope. And when the argument or moment of contention is over, you feel a sense of peace because you didn't react in the flesh. Because if you react in the flesh, guilt and shame quickens. So, being quiet or quoting scripture ensures that you are fighting fair. It ensures that, like Jesus, you are commanding peace in the storm.

So, I ask you again: are you fighting fair? When your coworker says something offhand, fight fair. When your spouse does something to upset you, fight fair. When someone brings up your past and tries to attack your purpose, fight fair. Our Great Dane knows that her "stature" is enough. I assure you, your "stature" (reputation by Christ) is enough. You don't need to show how big and tough you are, because being silent or responding with the Word speaks more volumes than what you can ever say. In fact, it actually reflects your "stature" more—that you are indeed walking with Jesus and are empowered by Him.

LaKeesha Griffin, God's pupil

Prayer

Lord, my Guide, I, (put your name here), thank you for living an exemplary life for me to model. I thank you for your Word, which is a lamp unto my feet and a light unto my path. It is the only reliable blueprint for every scenario I could ever face in life. I thank you that when I use your Word, I overcome the enemy. I repent, Lord, that I fail to respond to antagonism with silence or with your Word. I repent that I have not been quick to listen and slow to speak. Lord, I ask you to help me live a life exemplary of your life here on Earth. I ask you to help me hold my tongue and to bolster your

Kingdom by saying to others what is written in your Word. Now Lord, here I am, willing and able to do your will and be silent or speak your word when the time requires me to do so. In Jesus's name, Amen.

Application

1. Write the narrative, with dialogue, of the last fight you had.

2. Now, look at only your dialogue. Did your dialogue spark the fire, causing more discord?

3. Rewrite what would have been a better way to respond.

4. Considering your edited dialogue, do you think the disagreement would have ended differently if you had responded in that way?

5. Make a conscience effort to be silent or respond with the Word of God in the midst of confusion and aggression.

Make Notes Here:

Biblical Roots for Your Week

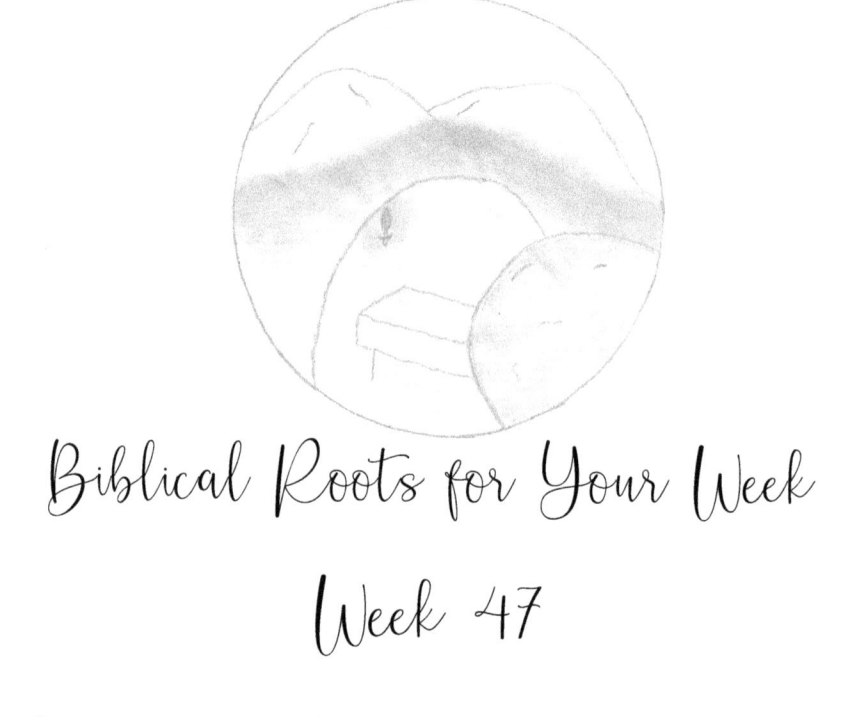

Week 47

The temple set upon the rock may sway, but never falls.

The Solid Rock

Our bodies are the House of the Lord. We know scripture tells us that the Holy Spirit dwells within us.[174] So, it is incumbent upon us to take care of our temples, making sure what goes in is Holy and righteous. Why? Because the Holy Spirit will not dwell in unclean places—"No one will get by with vandalizing God's temple, you can be sure of that. God's temple is sacred—and you, remember, are the temple."[175] But that's not what I want to explore with you.

---

[174] 1 Corinthians 3:16
[175] 1 Corinthians 3:16–17 (MSG)

We rarely talk about how, like a house, we, too, must weather the storm. Take just a moment and think about a house in the midst of a fierce storm. The rain is brutally beating up on it; the wind blows its rooftop shingles; its surrounding trees come tumbling down, crushing parts of the house; and the continual rain threatens the house with a flood. Now, think of yourself as that house, because in reality, you are. The trials of everyday life are brutally beating you down. What you thought was a safety net gets blown away, just like the rooftop shingles. Those friends who you thought would go through the fire with you turned out to tumble down right at the beginning of your storm, just as the trees on the house. And now, hopelessness seems to threaten the inside of your house (temple) just as the flood. But wait! What about the foundation?

Matthew 7:25 (KJV) teaches us that the rain will descend, the floods will come, and the winds will blow and beat upon the house. That scripture promises that this house (your temple) will not fall if its foundation was built right.[176] Well, how can the foundation keep the house from falling when there are all these outside threats that seem to be shaking the house (your temple)? The foundation keeps the house from falling because the house was founded upon a rock—Jesus. Jesus, in this scripture, compares Himself to a rock because a rock is deemed steady, strong, and durable. So, your house (temple) can't fall because it is built on what is steady, strong, and durable.

After the storm, when you go and assess the damage, be willing to cure some defects in your house, such as your choice of friends and what you relied on as a safety net, which probably shouldn't have been there in the first place.

---

[176] Matthew 7:24

I encourage you to look at your storms in life as a blessing to assess the damage of what is needless and destructive to your house (temple). And, as an added bonus, rest assured, the storm that vandalized your house (temple) will not get away with it.[177]

LaKeesha Griffin, God's pupil

Prayer

Lord, my Rock, I, (put your name here), thank you for being the steady foundation on which I stand. I thank you that though my house may tremble from the storms of life, it cannot fall. Lord, I thank you that you hold the keys to my house, being so kind as to show me when I need to clean house and remove those things which are destructive to my temple. Lord, I repent that the storms that beat upon my temple cause me to fear. I repent that because it feels like everything is falling out of place, I often react in despair. I realize now, Lord, that you cause those things to fall out of place so that I can assess what is destructive to my temple and needless to my spiritual growth. Lord, I ask you to help me see the storms of life as a blessing to assess my temple. I ask that you give me the courage to remove those people and things from my life that are a hindrance to my growth in your Kingdom. Now Lord, here I am, willing and able to do your will and clean my house. In Jesus's name, Amen.

Application

1. Conduct a self-assessment of your temple.

---

[177] 1 Corinthians 3:16–17 (MSG)

2. Now, in all honesty, what are some habits you have that are destructive to your temple?

3. Do you have any relationships you consider destructive to your temple?

4. Ask God for the courage to clean your house, removing any bad habits or people you listed as destructive to your temple.

5. Continue to conduct self-assessments anytime you experience a trial or struggle in life, then repeat the above steps.

Make Notes Here:

Biblical Roots for Your Week

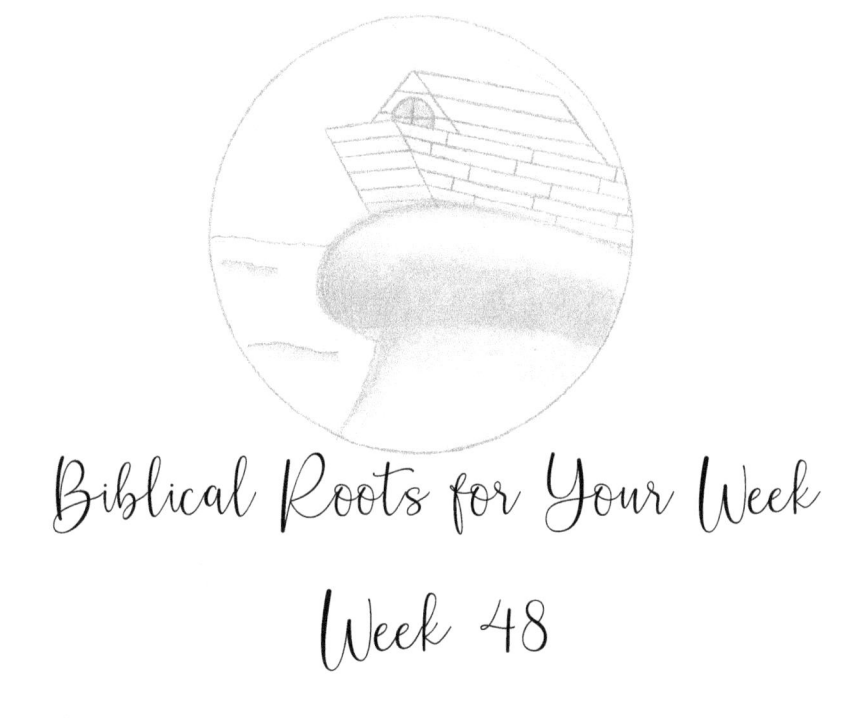

Week 48

My war cry is a signal to other troops to not forget that the battle has already been won.

Rally the Troops

At the onset of war, there is always a meeting of like minds with similar interests to plan to protect what they hold dear and love. It goes like this, and I am sure you have seen it portrayed in movies: the commander in-chief, in the middle of the night when most are sleeping, gets a call; all leaders are instructed to meet and will be briefed about the details at the meeting; there, after much deliberation, they make a uniform decision to take out the common enemy posing a threat to what they consider dear and love. Yes! You have probably guessed what happens next. They then "rally the troops." Our lives aren't any different. We have a common enemy with the ongoing plot to kill us, steal everything we hold dear and love, and destroy our hopes and future of an eternity with Jesus.[178] We are empowered by God to "rally the troops."

"Rallying the troops" means encouraging those who fight with you and alongside you to give it their absolute all. We who believe that the battle has already been won by our commander-in-chief, Jesus Christ, only have one duty as He continues to fight for us. We must perfect our war cry! You perfect your war cry by being intentional to call on those of like minds with similar interests to pray with you when you (and they) are facing imminent danger. The Word of God says that where two or three are gathered together in Jesus's name, the commander-in-chief, Jesus, is there also.[179] The presence of the commander-in-chief makes the difference because His presence reminds the enemy of his unending defeat.

Like all enemies, the devil feels a sense of confidence that he can conquer the territory that has already been claimed. Well, we are God's territory—being claimed even before our first breath—and His claim over us was made in perpetuity. Our assignment is then staying vigilant and sounding our war cry, because the enemy is unconvincing of his defeat and is prowling like a lion, seeking whom he may devour.[180] We remain vigilant by praying together. When we pray together, we shake things up and change the landscape, making it ever more difficult for the enemy to reach us: "And when they

---

[178] John 10:10
[179] Matthew 18:20
[180] 1 Peter 5:8 (NIV)

had prayed, the place was shaken where they were assembled together."[181]

I encourage you to sound the alarm. Send out your war cry when you face imminent danger. Never face the battle alone. "Rally the troops!"

LaKeesha Griffin, God's pupil

Prayer

Lord, the Commander-in-Chief, I, (put your name here), thank you that you have won the battle for my life. I thank you that your claim to my life never ends, and because of that, the enemy can never conquer my soul. Lord, thank you for assigning me a duty to get with like-minded believers to alert you that the enemy is prowling around your territory. I know that when I sound out my war cry, you are faithful to come to my rescue, and the enemy will retreat because he will be reminded of his unending defeat and lack of authority over my soul. Lord, I repent that I have not sought out other believers to help me sound the alarm when the enemy is on the prowl. When I feel like I am under attack, Father, I repress it for fear that others will see me as weak. Lord, please forgive me for that. Now I know, in my weakness, your strength prevails. I ask you to give me the courage to seek help from other believers so they can pray with me in my time of need. Now Lord, here I am, willing and able to do your will and rally the troops. In Jesus's name, Amen.

---

[181] Acts 4:31 (KJV)

Application

1. Make a list of those like-minded people whom you can call on any day or any hour.

2. Find a scripture that evokes the power of God over the enemy that you can say boldly to the enemy when you are under attack.

3. Write that scripture down as many times as you need to and place in each location that is a part of your regular routine (i.e., car, workplace, kitchen, bathroom, etc.).

4. Now say the scripture aloud and keep doing so every time you feel under attack by the enemy.

5. Don't forsake the power of prayer with others.

Make Notes Here:

Biblical Roots for Your Week

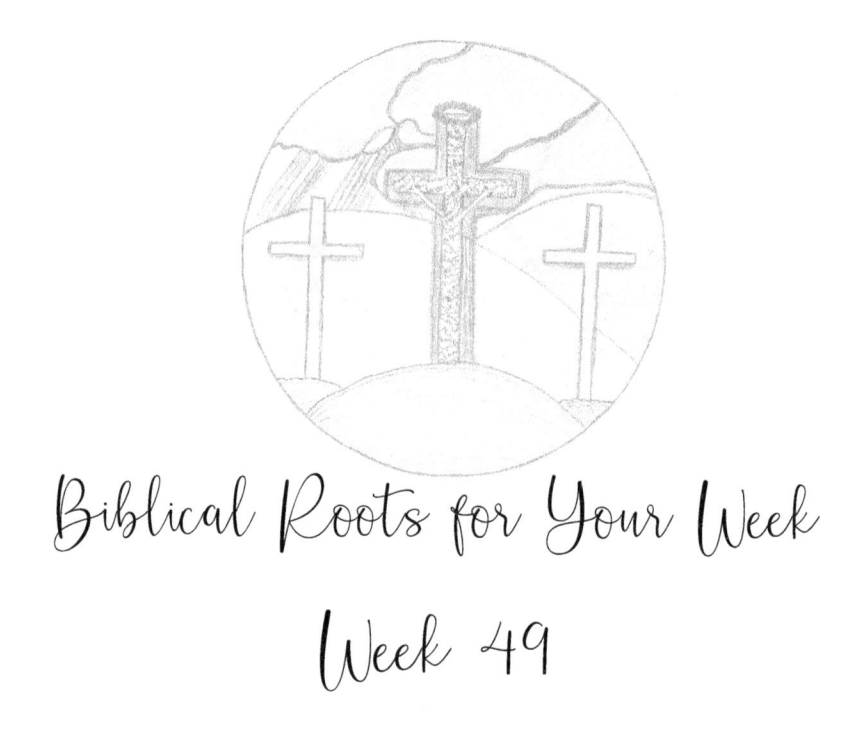

Week 49

Pain faced while holding God's hand heightens my faith and readies me for the next level.

Level Up

What do you do if you hit your head or stump your toe? Odds are, you walk to the freezer and put ice on your injury. We do this to numb the pain because sometimes, pain can be overbearing. The numbing sensation provides temporary relief from feeling the pain. As soon as the ice melts or we take the ice pack off our injury, the feeling of pain returns. In our Christian walk, pain—from heartbreak, disappointment, failures, and so on—should not be numbed. Don't get me wrong—neither of us wish to feel pain, and I do believe that God does not plan for us to go through pain: God has plans to prosper us, not to harm us, but to give us hope and a future.[182] However, He works the pain for our good.[183] But how does God work pain for our good?

God intends for us to feel the pain. Yes, you read that right. He wants us to feel the pain. When we feel the pain, we learn from it. It is when we feel the pain and then learn from it that we receive our elevation to the next level. Let's revisit heartbreak as an example. In our youth, we all have experienced some form of heartbreak, whether it was a boyfriend/girlfriend scenario, best friend crisis, or a loved one who let us down. When we experienced the heartbreak, we became guarded. People oftentimes think this to be a bad thing because it prevents one from being vulnerable; but, again, all things work for our good—"above all else, guard your heart, for everything you do flows from it."[184] Heartbreak teaches us qualities of trustworthiness, the importance of having standards, and that people are imperfect—that only God can live up to our ideals of real love.

Pain creates an environment for promotion, elevation, and growth. The Word of God teaches us that we become mature and complete because of our pain: "consider it pure joy, my brothers and sisters, whenever you face trials of many kinds, because you know that the testing of your faith produces perseverance. Let perseverance finish its work so that you may be mature and complete, not lacking anything."[185]

In a video game, there is always a monster/giant at the end of the level. But to defeat the monster/giant, you must

---

[182] Jeremiah 29:11 (NIV)
[183] Romans 8:28
[184] Proverbs 4:23 (NIV)
[185] James 1:1–4 (NIV)

face it head-on. If you prevail, you level up, advancing to the next level. If you do not prevail, you have to repeat the same level again until you reach victory over the monster/giant. Our life is no different. We must face our pain head-on to level up! Level up!!!

LaKeesha Griffin, God's pupil

Prayer

Lord, my Comforter, I, (put your name here), thank you that you console me when I suffer from pain in my life. I thank you that you recycle that pain and use it for my good by causing me to learn from it so my faith may be perfected. Lord, thank you for your plans for me to prosper. I realize part of that plan to give me a hope and a future includes me feeling pain so that I can learn from it. Lord, I repent that I have not perceived pain to be good by any means. I have always felt it to be an unnecessary evil in my life. However, now I see that you, though you did not plan for the pain, use the pain to help me grow so that I am ready for my next level. I ask you to help me to face my pain head-on instead of running from it. I ask you to help me defeat the giants on this level so I can receive elevation to the next level. Now Lord, here I am, willing and able to do your will and level up. In Jesus's name, Amen.

Application

1. What does the monster/giant look like at the end of this level in your life?

2. In your opinion, how can you defeat the monster/giant of this level?

3. Have you tried facing the monster/giant head-on?

4. Don't ignore the monster/giant in your life; ask God to help you face it head-on.

Make Notes Here:

Biblical Roots for Your Week

Week 50

The contract where I benefit, but I didn't sign my name, is only enforceable because Jesus signed with His blood.

The Third-Party Contract

Let's take a seat in a law school class for just a moment. In contract law, specific performance is an idea that all parties are bound to the terms of the contract. If one party does not specifically perform under the contract, the other party may be granted by a judge specific performance as a legal remedy. There are also third-party contracts: this is when someone (not a party to a contract) may be affected or benefit from the contract. This means the legal obligation to perform is on the one who agreed with their signature, and not the third party.

Man had a covenant, or a contract, with God. God had given man dominion over all things except for eating from the tree of knowledge of good and evil.[186] This is referred to as the Adamic Covenant (for the sake of our class, let's refer to it as the Adamic Contract). The Adamic Contract was indeed breached as Adam and Eve disobeyed God by eating from the forbidden tree.[187] As a result, God, the judge of the highest court, demanded specific performance as a legal remedy. However, man was unable to pay compensatory damages—to put humankind back in the place before the act which breached the contract took place, as if the breach had never occurred.

God, our most gracious judge, allowed for a third-party contract with Jesus (with God and Jesus as the contracting parties). He excluded us as a party to the contract entirely but makes us a beneficiary to the contract because man did not have the power nor authority to remedy the breach of the Adamic Contract. So Jesus entered the contract, signing it with His blood. Jesus made a blood oath—a commitment via His blood—swearing to specifically perform, as the blood signifies the penalty for man breaking the contract. In other words, this third-party contract's terms where written so that the blameless one (Jesus) would have to pay for man's breach of the Adamic Contract; Jesus had to suffer the penalty for the broken contract with His blood. The third party (us) now enjoys the benefit of a new contract, called the New Covenant: "This cup is the new Covenant in my blood. Which is poured out for you."[188]

---

[186] Genesis 1:26–30; 2:16–17
[187] Genesis 3:6–19
[188] Luke 22:20 (NIV)

Thank the Lord for the legal remedy of specific performance, not performed by man, but by Jesus on the Cross for us—the third party to the New Covenant. Hallelujah!

LaKeesha Griffin, God's pupil

Prayer

Lord, the Judge of the Highest Court, I, (put your name here), thank you that you judge with grace and mercy. I thank you that you devised an alternative route for humankind to get back to you. Thank you, Father, for making a third-party contract with Jesus so that I may benefit from the blood He shed on the Cross. I declare your lovingkindness never fails. Lord, I repent for taking the price you paid for man's breach of contract for granted. I repent for not having joy in my heart that I get to benefit at the price of Jesus's blood. I ask you to keep me reminded of the price He paid to specifically perform under the New Covenant. Jesus, thank you for pouring out your blood for me. Now Lord, here I am, willing and able to do your will and be grateful of the benefits Jesus's blood afforded me. In Jesus's name, Amen.

Application

1. Make a list of benefits you seldom think about as a benefit.

2. Have you ever breached (broken) an agreement you made with someone?

3. What would it have taken to remedy your broken agreement, placing the person back in the place they were before you broke the agreement?

4. Now, meditate on Jesus placing himself in your stead for every broken agreement you could ever make.

5. Describe what would have resulted if Jesus did not put humankind back in the place before man broke the agreement with God.

6. Stay grateful of Jesus's sacrifice.

Make Notes Here:

Biblical Roots for Your Week

Week 51

I receive unending gifts I am unworthy of but qualify for because I am a child of God.

Free Gifts

"Present" is a multiple meaning word. It could mean either that someone or something is in a particular place, or someone or something is existing or occurring now (hence our usage in grammar of the "present" tense). But there is one more meaning of "present," and that is to give or award, or to "gift."

God has fulfilled every sense of the word "present." He promises that He will always be in a particular place. What place? Well, wherever we are. Joshua 1:9 (NIV) says, "For the Lord your God will be with you wherever you go." Deuteronomy 31:6 says, "He will never leave you nor forsake you." He is also a God that exists in our right now, for the Word says, "He has risen from the dead."[189] Jesus said, "I am alive for evermore . . . and I have the keys of Hell and of death."[190] The Word also says that He is a "very *present* help in trouble."[191] Lastly, He also fulfills the meaning of "present" because He gave His only begotten Son to you and me with hope that we would believe in Him and experience the free "gift" (or present) of eternal life.[192]

But God is a God of "et cetera," which means "and so forth" or "and other things." Not only do we who believe in him get to experience the "gift" of eternal life, we get to experience bits of heaven on our way. God renews His "gift" of His merciful love to us every morning.[193] So be encouraged that our God is present in every sense of the word.

Right where you are, He is present! Don't be discouraged! He is not dead, He is alive! So enjoy the "gifts" He bestows upon you! His love faileth not! For every good and perfect "gift" is from our Father in Heaven.[194]

LaKeesha Griffin, God's pupil

Prayer

Lord, My Very Present Help, My Gift of Eternal Life, I, (put your name here), thank you that you never leave me nor

---

[189] Matthew 28:6 (NIV)
[190] Revelation 1:18 (KJV)
[191] Psalm 46:1 (KJV)
[192] John 3:16
[193] Lamentations 3:23
[194] James 1:17

forsake me. I thank you that your presence is with me right now. I thank you that because you are present with me, you know my anxious thoughts. And I thank you that you are rescuing me from a path of destruction and placing me back on a righteous path. Lord, I ask that you send me reminders that you are here with me. Just like you are always present with me, Lord, I want to be also present with you. I want what I do, what I say, and what I think to be a sign from you that you are present with me in all that I do. Lord, I know I have failed you in my thoughts and actions. I repent now that I have focused too much on the environmental conditions than on you as my very present help in time of trouble. Trouble trembles at your name, Father. So, as I repent, Lord, I ask that you renew my mind and create a steadfast spirit within me to walk and talk with you continually. Now, Lord, here I am, willing and able to do your will and allow your presence to reign within my life. In Jesus's name, Amen.

Application

1. Make a list of the present manifestations you have in your life that prove God is present with you.

2. Write those manifestations on sticky notes and put them in places you frequent, such as your bathroom mirror, car, and so on.

3. Write a list of the trending events/circumstances that cause you to lose focus on God being with you wherever you are.

4. Be intentional when those events arise to revisit your list of manifestations that He is with you and is your very present help in times of trouble.

Make Notes Here:

Biblical Roots for Your Week

Week 52

It is ill-advised to attempt to fly high when ill-equipped for the journey.

Stages of Faith

A butterfly must go through four stages to reach maturity: 1. egg; 2. caterpillar (larva); 3. chrysalis (pupa); and 4. adult butterfly. The stages of a butterfly are analogous to the stages of our faith. In the early parts of our life (egg), we are immature in our faith. We often are just going through the routine of going to church—if we were fortunate enough to have someone take us there—and are totally dependent on the prayers of others because we have not had enough experience to know the true meaning of a relationship with God. Then, as we become older (caterpillar), we are introduced to heartaches and pain. In this stage, we have two choices: do what the caterpillar does, or refuse to do what the caterpillar does.

In the "caterpillar" stage, the caterpillar's main job is to eat in order to propel it into its next stage. If it refuses to do this adequately, there is no hope for it becoming mature. In other words, if it does not eat enough in the caterpillar stage, it will never become an adult butterfly. Likewise, if we respond to the heartache and pain in our lives by refusing to chew on the Word of God, we never reach full maturity—"My people are destroyed for lack of knowledge."[195] We must respond to our heartache and pain with eagerness to draw closer to the Word of God; we are instructed to delight in the Word of God, chewing it for spiritual nourishment every day and night.[196] Delighting in the Word of God does not make you immune to heartache and pain; instead, it gives you a deeper understanding of it. But be ready, because now that you are delighting in the Word of God, you will be bombarded with more trials and struggles—and therefore, more heartache and pain. Why?

The devil ramps up his attempts against you because he doesn't want the Word of God to be deposited in your heart. Before it can take root in your heart, "Satan cometh immediately, and taketh away the Word that was sown in [your] heart."[197] He does this by reintroducing old issues you thought you'd overcome, attacking your character, or using someone close to you to disappoint you; the list is unending.

---

[195] Hosea 4:6
[196] Psalm 1:2
[197] Mark 4:15 (KJV)

Often, we respond to Satan's attempts to deter us from the Word of God by deterring ourselves from the Word of God. We retreat in our own cocoons (chrysalis), taking on the world by ourselves and failing to delight ourselves in the Law of the Lord: the Word of God.[198] But God penetrates our cocoons. He pursues us and places within our hearts how we are to be healed—by coming to Jesus, the Word of God. "No one can come to me unless the Father who sent me draws them, and I will raise them up at the last day."[199]

When we reach a breaking point, finally having learned from all of our previous stages of life, we learn that the remedy to all our woes is always Jesus, the Word of God. Jesus then makes us mature by causing us to crave the Word of God—"Like newborn babies, crave spiritual milk, so that by it you may grow up in your salvation."[200] Now, mature in Christ—He causes us to soar (as an adult butterfly) to new heights in our faith.

I encourage you to draw closer to the Word of God. It is there that you find the answer to your life's qualms. I leave you with this: "all scripture is God-breathed and is useful for teaching, rebuking, correcting, and training in righteousness, so that the servant of God may be thoroughly equipped for every good work."[201] I implore you to equip yourself to fly to new heights by reading, meditating, and applying the Word of God!

LaKeesha Griffin, God's pupil

---

[198] Psalm 1:2
[199] John 6:44 (NIV)
[200] 1 Peter 2:2 (NIV)
[201] 2 Timothy 3:16–17 (NIV)

Prayer

Lord, the Word of Truth, I, (put your name here), thank you that you breathed your Word into man so that I may have a manuscript for how to conduct my life. I thank you that your Word equips me with everything for this life so I may live eternally with you in my next life. Lord, I thank you that you are patient with me on my journey to arrive at a stage of maturity, whereby I will look to your Word for direction. And, mostly, I am grateful to you for always pursuing me, causing me to draw toward you. It is you alone who makes my heart fertile to receive your Word so it is deposited in my heart forever. Lord, I repent that I have been stagnant on my Christian journey. I have failed to chew on your Word so it will nourish my soul and grow me into an adult butterfly. Lord, I ask you to help me to wholeheartedly, without any reservations, receive your Word in my heart and to apply it and soar to new heights. I ask you to make me who I am destined to be. I realize I will never get there unless I search for you in your Word and find myself—my purpose, value, gifts, talents, and identity—in your Word. Thank you for your Word that is working to create me anew. Now Lord, here I am, willing and able to do your will and do what your Word instruct me to do. In Jesus's name, Amen.

Application

1. What stage of your faith walk are you in? 1) Egg; 2) Caterpillar (Larva); 3. Chrysalis (Pupa); or 4. Adult butterfly.

2. Why are you in that stage?

3. How often do you read the Word of God?

4. Are you taking time to meditate on the Word of God?

5. Are you taking time to hear from God on how the scripture(s) you read apply to your life for teaching, rebuking, correcting, and training in righteousness?

6. Be intentional to ask God in prayer how the scripture(s) you read apply to your life; when you hear from Him, be willing to make the changes to become mature in Christ (an adult butterfly).

Make Notes Here:

Reference sources

Scripture quotations taken from the Amplified® Bible (AMP), Copyright © 2015 by The Lockman Foundation. Used by permission. www.lockman.org

Scripture quotations from The Authorized (King James) Version. Rights in the Authorized Version in the United Kingdom are vested in the Crown. Reproduced by permission of the Crown's patentee, Cambridge University Press. BFBS additions. Copyright 1954, 2011 by British and Foreign Bible Society.

Scripture taken from The Message. Copyright © 1993, 1994, 1995, 1996, 2000, 2001, 2002. Used by permission of NavPress Publishing Group.

Scripture quotations taken from the (NASB®) New American Standard Bible®, Copyright © 1960, 1962, 1963, 1968, 1971, 1972, 1973, 1975, 1977, 1995, 2020 by The Lockman Foundation. Used by permission. All rights reserved. www.lockman.org

Scripture quotations taken from the Holy Bible, New International Versions®, NIV® Copyright © 1973, 1978, 1984, 2011 by Biblica, Inc. Used with permission. All rights reserved worldwide.

Life Application® Study Bible, New International Version®. Copyright 1988, 1989, 1990, 1991, 2005 by Tyndale House Publishers, Inc.

Scripture taken from the New King James Version®. Copyright © 1982 by Thomas Nelson. Used by permission. All rights reserved."

BFBS additions. Copyright 1954, 2011 by British and Foreign Bible Society.

Other Reference Sources

Evans, Jimmy. The Four Laws of Love: Guaranteed Success for Every Married Couple. XO Publishing, 2019.

Houghton, Israel. "Jesus At the Center." Jesus at the Center: Live. Integrity Music, 2012. CD.

OED Online, Oxford University Press, © 2022, www.oed.com. Accessed November 2020 – September 2022.